RAISE THE
ISSUES

RAISE THE ISSUES

An Integrated Approach to Critical Thinking

Third Edition

Carol Numrich

In Cooperation with NPR®

PEARSON
Longman

Raise the Issues: An Integrated Approach to Critical Thinking, Third Edition

Copyright © 2010, 2002 by Pearson Education, Inc.
All rights reserved.

Pearson Education, 10 Bank Street, White Plains NY, 10606

Staff credits: The people who made up the *Raise the Issues, Third Edition* team, representing editorial, production, design, and manufacturing, are John Barnes, Dave Dickey, Ann France, Shelley Gazes, Amy McCormick, Carlos Rountree, and Jennifer Stem.

Cover art: George Marks/Getty Images
Text composition: Word and Image Design Studio, Inc.
Text font: 11.5/13 Minion

Art credits: **Page 1**, http://www.cartoonstock.com/; **Page 19**, http://www.cartoonstock.com/; **Page 42**, © The New Yorker Collection 1997 William Hamilton from cartoonbank.com. All Rights Reserved.; **Page 64**, http://www.cartoonstock.com/; **Page 85**, © The New Yorker Collection 1997 Boris Drucker from cartoonbank.com. All Rights Reserved.; **Page 103**, © The New Yorker Collection 2006 J.B. Handelsman from cartoonbank.com. All Rights Reserved.; **Page 125**, http://www.cartoonstock.com/; **Page 145**, © The New Yorker Collection 2000 Jack Ziegler from cartoonbank.com. All Rights Reserved.; **Page 163**, © The New Yorker Collection 1988 William Steig from cartoonbank.com. All Rights Reserved.; **Page 184**, John Cole.

National Public Radio, NPR, *All Things Considered*, *Day to Day*, *Morning Edition* and their logos are registered and unregistered service marks of National Public Radio, Inc.

Library of Congress Cataloging-in-Publication Data

Numrich, Carol.
    Raise the issues : an integrated approach to critical thinking / Carol Numrich;
    in cooperation with NPR.—3rd ed.
        p. cm.
    ISBN-13: 978-0-13-700730-1 (pbk.)
    ISBN-10: 0-13-700730-2 (pbk.)
    1. English language—Textbooks for foreign speakers. 2. Critical thinking—Problems, exercises, etc. I. National Public Radio (U.S.) II. Title.
    PE1128.N85 2009
    428.2'4--dc22

                                                                    2009008813

ISBN-10: 0-13-700730-2
ISBN-13: 978-0-13-700730-1

Printed in the United States of America
8 9 10—V011—14

CONTENTS

SCOPE AND SEQUENCE

READING	SPEAKING	WRITING
"Unsafe at Any Speed" *Marek Fuchs*	Group discussion: A case of child endangerment	Using simple present for past narratives Writing narrative essays
"The Trouble with Single-Sex Schools" *Wendy Kaminer*	Role play: Addressing single-sex traditions on the college campus	Using noun clauses Using parallel structure
"Can Buy Me Love? Why the Private Choice of Adoption has International Consequences" *Ivy George*	Group discussion: On serving the needs of the children of international adoptions	Using subjects and verbs correctly to achieve agreement Writing introductions and conclusions
"All for the Good: Why Genetic Engineering Must *Soldier On*" *James D. Watson*	Group discussion: Deciding to participate in genetic research	Using count and non-count nouns Writing cohesive paragraphs
"The Disappearing Scholar-Athlete (Colleges Should Not Sacrifice Education to Sports)" *New York Times staff writer*	Group discussion: The proper place of sports and athletes in higher education	Using the passive voice Writing argumentative essays
"Ángels in America" *John Tierney*	Debate: Should illegal immigrants be granted amnesty?	Using comparison structures Writing comparison essays
"More on When to Die" *William F. Buckley, Jr.*	Debate: The pros and cons of legal doctor-assisted suicide	Using participial phrases Making concessions in opinion essays
"Are We Coming Apart or Together?" *Pico Iyer*	Group discussion: Judging an anti-globalization leader	Using the double comparative Illustrating with examples
"Sure There's a Price, but It Pays to Play" *Ronald Grover*	Role play: Studying the economic and social effects of gambling	Using adjective clauses Understanding idioms
"Biofuel Myths" *Eric Holt-Giménez*	Group discussion: On a sustainable energy future and the impact of biofuels	Using implied conditions Writing argumentative essays using refutations

INTRODUCTION

Raise the Issues: An Integrated Approach to Critical Thinking, Third Edition, consists of ten authentic radio commentaries from National Public Radio; articles or essays excerpted from a variety of magazines, journals, and newspapers; and related exercises.

Designed for very advanced students of English as a second language, the book presents an integrated approach to developing critical thinking skills. Each unit explores a controversial issue of international appeal. Students gain an understanding of American values and attitudes as they develop their listening and reading skills. They begin to reevaluate their assumptions and form their own points of view as they develop their speaking and writing skills. By using material designed for the native speaker, the listening and reading selections provide authentic content that is interesting, relevant, and educational.

The third edition of *Raise the Issues* offers five new units. Variety in exercises has been introduced to several units, including new listening comprehension tasks, alternative activities for synthesizing the listening and reading material, and new vocabulary exercises.

SUGGESTIONS FOR USE

The exercises are designed to stimulate an interest in the material by drawing on students' previous knowledge and opinions and by aiding comprehension through vocabulary and guided listening and reading exercises. In a variety of discussion activities, students integrate new information and concepts with previously held opinions. In the writing exercises, students are given an opportunity to explore the issues further and use the new language and insights gained.

I. Anticipating the Issue

In this two- to three-minute introductory discussion, students predict what the issue will be and share whatever knowledge of the topic they may already have. The title, cartoon, and questions are meant to introduce the content of the unit and motivate students to read further. The ideas generated by the discussion could be written on the board. After reading the Background Reading, students can verify or react to their predictions. The teacher may want to provide additional information to help students understand the cartoon or issue.

II. Background Reading

Background Reading: The Background Reading has two purposes: to provide students with facts and cultural information that will help them comprehend the opinion pieces that follow, and to introduce the vocabulary that they will need to understand the recorded radio commentary (Opinion 1). The Background

Reading takes no position but rather presents two sides of the issue. Students should read the text silently in class.

Vocabulary: The Background Reading in each unit is followed by an exercise to reinforce the difficult or topic-specific vocabulary presented. The exercise types include guessing meaning from context, working with synonyms, defining words, and completing sentences.

Summarizing the Issue: This activity will help students check their understanding of the issues presented in the Background Reading. In groups, students discuss their interpretation of the main issue. Then they are asked to identify the main arguments made by each side of the issue.

Values Clarification: Before listening to and reading the opinions of others, students discuss, in groups, their own reactions to or opinions about the issue. This discussion should increase their interest and understanding of the issues and prepare them for the opinion pieces that follow. Studying the opinions of others promotes critical thinking and requires students to reconsider their original assumptions and opinions.

III. Opinion 1: Listening

Listening for the Main Idea: Students should listen to the commentary once through without stopping. They then answer questions that focus on the commentator's main idea. Students may compare their answers in pairs to see whether they have understood the essential point(s) of the commentary. Only one listening is usually required for this exercise, but some classes may want to listen a second time. The teacher may want to ask the class why any incorrect answers do not represent the main idea.

Listening for Details: Students listen to the commentary again. Here they answer multiple-choice questions, analyze true/false statements, write short answers, complete statements, or categorize concepts to help them understand and distinguish detailed information. Students should first read the questions and, where appropriate, the possible answers. The teacher can then explain any items that students do not understand. Then the commentary is played. Students answer questions *as they listen*, thus evaluating their listening comprehension while listening. Finally, in pairs, they compare answers. In comparing and defending their answers, students should be encouraged to use the language from the radio commentary to persuade the other students of the accuracy of their choices. There will certainly be disagreements over some of the answers; these discussions will help focus attention on the information needed to answer the questions correctly. After listening to the commentary a second time, students generally comprehend this information and agree on their answers. If there are still disagreements, the commentary might be played a third time, with the teacher verifying the answers and pointing out where the information is heard.

Text Completion and Discrete Listening: In this final listening activity, students fill in the missing words from the listening passage. This cloze-type exercise focuses on topic-specific vocabulary or discrete grammatical forms students have heard, and presents the commentary in writing. Students should complete this exercise using their knowledge of vocabulary, text structure, and the issue as well as their memory of what they have heard. (Note: This is not intended as a dictation.) Once students have filled in the blanks, the teacher can play the commentary again to verify their answers. Students' alternative answers can then be examined in a class discussion. The completion exercise could also be assigned as homework.

IV. Opinion 2: Reading

Reading for the Main Idea(s): Each unit presents an authentic reading selected from a variety of current periodicals and journals. These selections appear in their original form or only slightly edited for length and comprehensibility. Each reading presents a different, and sometimes opposite, point of view to that presented in the commentary. In some cases glosses have been included to explain unusual terms or phrases.

In this exercise, students identify the author's thesis by selecting main idea statements or answering questions on the author's point of view. To do this, students must separate the essential ideas from the less relevant or extraneous information. They must also distinguish the author's opinions from the opinions of others discussed in the text.

Students can compare their answers in pairs or groups, and the teacher can discuss any points that students do not understand. The teacher may want to assign the reading passage and reading exercises as homework.

Reading for Details: Once students have agreed on the author's main idea, the focus moves to the details the author uses to support the main idea. A variety of comprehension exercises encourage students' understanding of these details. Students may answer specific detail questions, select from multiple-choices, or analyze true-false statements. The answers to these exercises are not always "black and white." Students explore the "gray area" of less literal meaning. Students should be permitted to disagree with answers in the answer key *if* they can provide convincing arguments for their own opinions.

In some cases, students decide whether the statements presented would be supported by the author. Here they are asked to "read between the lines" to comprehend the finer distinctions of the author's point of view. They must distinguish between when an author is discussing the views of others and when he or she is presenting his or her own opinion.

In another alternative, students are given statements made by the author of the text, but they must distinguish facts from opinions. Students will discover that authors tend to use a combination of facts and opinions in writing, and through this process will come to realize the benefit of using both in their own writing.

Word Search: This is a vocabulary reinforcement exercise that works well as a homework exercise or as an in-class supplementary exercise for students who finish the comprehension exercises early. The teacher should emphasize that although a word may have more than one meaning in a dictionary, only the meaning that has been used by the author is given in this exercise. Once students have read the words in the context of the reading, they review vocabulary through a variety of exercises: selecting the best synonym or definition for each word or phrase in a multiple-choice exercise, clarifying meaning by completing sentences, or matching words or phrases with synonyms that have been grouped according to parts of speech (nouns, verbs, adjectives), which helps students focus on how the words are normally used in sentences.

V. Synthesizing Two Opinion Pieces

Distinguishing Opinions: In this activity, students are asked to compare and contrast the views of the commentator and the author. A variety of exercises accomplishes this goal: locating opposing viewpoints in the text, matching contrasting quotes on particular themes, categorizing contrasting views according to theme, and writing letters between different people to express opposing views. Because this evaluation involves a high level of student interpretation, no answer key is given. In discussing the author's or commentator's views, students may disagree and go back to the two texts to locate information that supports their answers. The teacher may want to guide this activity with a particular answer in mind but should remain open to the arguments that students give for their own answers.

Through their group discussion, students should come to realize that the commentator and author might agree on certain points and disagree on others. They will see that the different stances taken on an issue are not always in direct opposition, that issues are more complex than that. They will realize that in disagreement there is usually an area in which people may agree. This should help students examine a dispute from a variety of viewpoints. They can then begin to take their own position on the issue.

Giving Your Opinion: Once students have distinguished the viewpoints of the commentator and author, they express their own opinions by reacting to those viewpoints. This exercise can also be used as an optional discussion for groups that finish the previous exercise early.

Vocabulary Reinforcement: Combining vocabulary from both the commentary and article or essay, this exercise reinforces students' comprehension of words and phrases that were studied in earlier exercises. It asks students to apply or analyze the vocabulary they have studied in a new context. There are a variety of exercise types, including categorization, concept grids, word form identification, word relations, and sentence writing.

VI. Speaking

The teacher may want to choose to do one of the speaking activities. These exercises promote communication in the context of decision making. The exercises require students to draw on all the material presented in the unit and apply their opinions and those of others to specific cases or questions.

Case Study: The case studies in each of the units are true stories from the news. The case study has been written as a summary, incorporating some of the vocabulary and issues presented in the unit. The students are asked to weigh the arguments presented in the case and ultimately make a decision.

The activities presented in each case vary. In all units, the students first read the case study. Then a role play, debate, or group discussion follows.

Discussion Questions: These questions can be used to guide a class discussion or a small-group discussion. The questions seek to guide students to an important stage of critical thinking—coming to their own conclusions on the issue.

VII. Writing

Grammar: Each unit focuses on a grammatical structure used in the commentary, the opinion reading, or both. These structures have been chosen to respond to the advanced learner's needs in developing more sophisticated forms in writing. Students review a particular grammar point in the context in which it was presented. They predict how the particular grammar point is formed and used, and then review various rules and explanations for the grammar. Finally, they practice the grammar point in a structured exercise. (The teacher may want to supplement this section with other sources, as the explanations are not intended to be all-inclusive.)

Writing Style: This exercise focuses on an interesting and useful style of writing used in the commentary, the opinion reading, or both. Again, these excerpts have been chosen for their relevance to the advanced learner's needs in developing a more sophisticated style in writing. Students review a segment of writing. Using guided questions, they explore the particular style of writing. They then read an explanation for how or why the style is used. Finally, they complete an exercise or short writing assignment to practice the style.

Essay Questions: This final exercise represents a culminating activity for the unit. The teacher may want to give the essay as a weekend writing assignment. The questions have been designed to elicit students' own opinions that they have developed throughout the course of the unit. At least one of the questions asked is argumentative in nature. Students should develop their own theses in answering the question. They should also be encouraged to refer to ideas expressed in the readings and commentary and practice using the language (vocabulary, grammar, and writing style) presented in the unit.

ACKNOWLEDGMENTS

I would like to thank my level 8/9 students at the American Language Program, Columbia University, who have provided me with such important feedback on the content and activities of this book during its various stages of development. Their contributions have been invaluable.

The editors and staff at Longman continue to believe in my work and have offered me sustained guidance and support through the development of each edition. I am particularly indebted to Amy McCormick, who provided much support in conceptualizing the third edition, and John Barnes, who gave me wonderful advice throughout the development process. Many folks from Longman contributed to this text in previous editions and should not be forgotten. Joanne Dresner, Debbie Sistino, Paula Van Ells, Sherry Preiss, and Eleanor Barnes all provided me with helpful advice and encouragement in the early stages, and I remain appreciative of all their contributions.

The staff at National Public Radio has continued to provide much support from the idea stage to the production stage. I am indebted to Leslie Sanders, Project Manager at NPR, for supporting the development of this third edition and helping with permissions. Amy DeCicco was extremely helpful in helping me research commentaries for the new edition. As always, Wendy Blair did a superb job of producing the accompanying audio program, and Frank Stasio's voice pulled it all together! Thanks to Wendy and Frank for their consistent best-quality production.

Finally, I could not have written a third edition of this book without the support of Eric, Justin, and Haley, who give me the inspiration to keep going.

Carol Numrich

Enforcing the Law

http://www.cartoonstock.com

I. ANTICIPATING THE ISSUE

Discuss your answers to the questions.

1. Look at the title. Look at the cartoon. What do you think the issue of this unit will be?

2. Do you know of existing laws that *are not* enforced but *should be*? Give examples.

3. Do you know of existing laws that *are* enforced but *should not be*? Give examples.

Read the text.

Just because a law is "on the books" does not mean that it is necessarily respected by the public or enforced by the authorities. Everyone knows of laws that exist but are consistently broken, the so-called meaningless laws. And then there are laws that are outdated or unnecessary for today's world. They no longer **bear resemblance to** people's current behavior or they seem ridiculous to people who live their lives sensibly.

Every day laws are broken, but authorities turn a blind eye to those who break them. People hire illegal immigrants to clean their houses, tend their yards, and care for their children. Groups of friends and colleagues bet money on sports teams, even though there are laws that prohibit gambling. Pedestrians cross the street when the light is red, but a jaywalker is rarely issued a **fine**. Traffic laws are perhaps the most ignored and unenforced laws on the books. Every day we see more cars speeding down highways than cars driving the speed limit. Although the law **stipulates** that cars must pass in the left lane, drivers often pass on the right. We see more and more harried drivers running red lights in spite of the fact that this is a serious traffic **violation**. What is less common to see is **cops** pulling these drivers over. Police officers could be **detaining** many drivers who break the law. One wonders why laws that could help save lives are not more strictly enforced.

On the other hand, there are many silly laws still on the books that are not relevant to today's world. For example, in Brainerd, Minnesota, a law states that every man is obliged to grow a beard. In West Virginia, children are not allowed to go to school with onions on their breath. In Pocatello, Idaho, it is against the law to make threatening or depressed faces as you walk around town, while in New York you may not place your thumb against the tip of your nose and wiggle your fingers at someone! Many of our laws were passed for a particular reason, in a particular context, during a particular period of time, but they have never been changed. So, do not travel to Brainerd, Minnesota, without a beard. You could be arrested!

In addition to such outdated laws, there are many current laws that seem to exist because some people do not use their common sense. Many of these laws involve the treatment of animals. In Tennessee, for example, it is illegal for any person to import, possess, or sell a skunk. The **Humane** Society in Florida prohibits the confinement of pigs during pregnancy. It is illegal to enclose a pregnant pig in a space where it may not turn around freely. (An exception to this law is made, however, if the pig is undergoing a medical examination by a **veterinarian**. Only while visiting a **vet** may a pregnant pig be confined!) In Alaska, you do not have to be a skilled hunter to shoot a bear; even **amateurs** can carry a gun and protect themselves from such danger. However, Alaskan law prohibits anyone from awakening a sleeping bear! If you find yourself **craving** caffeine while driving with your pet in your car, you had better not make even a quick coffee stop. In many states, bills are now being passed to make it a crime to leave pets in unattended cars under conditions that **pose a danger** to the animals. For example, when the temperature outside is only 56 degrees, the temperature inside a car can

soar to 86—30 degrees warmer. People could be **subject to** a fine up to $500 and as much as six months in jail if they leave their pets in a car. However, if people simply used their common sense, laws like this would not be necessary.

Laws are meant to protect us and ensure proper behavior in society, but perhaps we have gone too far in maintaining laws that no longer fit the world we live in or creating laws that no one respects.

A. VOCABULARY

Match the boldfaced words and phrases in the Background Reading with their definitions below. Write the word or phrase next to its definition. There are two matches for one of the definitions.

1. _____ : money you have to pay as a punishment

2. _____ : people who are not skillful at a particular activity

3. _____ : police officers

4. _____ : increase quickly to a high level

5. _____ : be similar to or look like someone or something else

6. _____ : having an extremely strong desire for something

7. _____ : treating people or animals in a way that is kind, not cruel

8. _____ : says that something must be done

9. _____ : likely to be affected by something, especially something bad

10. _____ : someone who is trained to give medical care and treatment to sick animals

11. _____ : an action that breaks a law

12. _____ : officially preventing someone from leaving a place

13. _____ : put something in a risky, dangerous situation

B. SUMMARIZING THE ISSUE

Work in small groups. Take notes on the two issues with law enforcement described in the Background Reading. Summarize the issues.

1. Laws that *are not* enforced but *should be*: _____

_____

_____

2. Laws that *are* enforced but *should not be*: _____

_____

_____

C. VALUES CLARIFICATION

Work in small groups. Discuss your answers to the questions.

1. Are driving laws typically ignored where you live? Discuss your observations of driving behavior and whether law enforcement is an issue.

2. Do animals need special laws to protect them? If so, give examples.

III. OPINION 1: LISTENING

A. LISTENING FOR THE MAIN IDEA

Listen to the commentary. Check the statement that best summarizes the commentator's main idea.

❏ 1. Dogs should never be left in a car, not even for a few minutes.

❏ 2. Animals need to be protected more by people who can educate others.

❏ 3. People who enforce the law should be more reasonable.

B. LISTENING FOR DETAILS

Listen again and complete the statements on the next page. For each statement, two answers are correct and one answer is incorrect. Cross out the incorrect answer. Compare your answers with those of another student. Listen again if necessary.

1. When commentator Daniel Pinkwater goes for a cappuccino, his car
   _____.
   a. has a temperature of 45 degrees inside
   b. is left with an open sunroof
   c. is being pulled away

2. _____ comes to Pinkwater's car to inform him that he is
   breaking the law.
   a. The vet
   b. The sheriff's deputy
   c. The humane law enforcement officer

3. It's a violation to leave a dog unattended in a car because _____.
   a. temperatures can soar
   b. the dog can die
   c. the temperatures are never cool

4. If you leave a dog in a car for just one minute, you _____.
   a. are fine
   b. are subject to a fine
   c. could be arrested

5. The humane enforcement officer wants to _____ Pinkwater.
   a. arrest
   b. educate
   c. inform

6. The officer tells Pinkwater that he may *not* let his dogs out to _____.
   a. spend more time than it takes to relieve themselves[1]
   b. romp on his property
   c. go into a bungalow

7. The supervisor _____.
   a. backs up what the officer said
   b. decides not to detain them
   c. tells them anecdotes about his career

8. Pinkwater is finally able to get away by telling the supervisor he is doing a
   great job _____.
   a. protecting animals
   b. educating the public
   c. downloading Section 353-B of Article 26

9. The experience leaves Pinkwater _____.
   a. craving closure
   b. paying money
   c. hating amateurs

---

[1]*relieve themselves:* go to the bathroom

C. TEXT COMPLETION AND DISCRETE LISTENING

Read the commentary. Fill in the prepositions. Then listen again to check your answers. If your answers differ from the commentary, ask your teacher if they are acceptable alternatives.

Introduction

Recently, the law caught up with commentator Daniel Pinkwater. It happened while he and his wife were out and about with their dogs.

Commentary

So Jill and I decide to duck _____ Antonella's _____ a cappuccino after
$~~~~~~$**1**$~~~~~~~~~~~~~~~~~~~~~~~~~~~~~~~~~$**2**

taking our dogs _____ the vet nearby. We leave the dogs _____ the car.
$~~~~~~~~~~~~~~~~~~~~~~~~~~~$**3**$~~~~~~$**4**

The dashboard temperature thing indicates that it's 45 degrees, and we leave the

sunroof open. We do this all the time. Suddenly, the vet is _____ the
$~~~~~~$**5**

restaurant. "Better get outside fast. Your dogs, your car." I rush outside. The

sheriff's deputy who made the call is just pulling away, and a humane law

enforcement officer is just getting out _____ her van.
$~~~~~~$**6**

　　"It is a violation _____ law to leave dogs unattended _____ a car. The
$~~~~~~~~~~~~~~~~~~~~~~~~~~~~~~$**7**$~~~~~~$**8**

temperature can soar. They can die." "I'm well aware _____ that, officer, but
$~~~~~~$**9**

it's 11 A.M. _____ a cool morning. The sunroof is open. The dogs are fine." "It
$~~~~~~~~~~~~~~~~~$**10**

doesn't matter," the officer says. "The new law stipulates that if you leave your dog

_____ the car _____ even one minute, you are subject _____ fine
11$~~~~~~~~~~~~~~~~~~~~~~$**12**$~~~~~~$**13**

and a possible arrest." "What? You mean, I can't even leave the dog _____ the
$~~~~~~$**14**

car while I pick up the dry cleaning? What law is this?" "Section 353-B _____
$~~~~~~$**15**

Article 26 of the New York State Agriculture and Markets Law. A car is not

considered an appropriate shelter."

　　I get the officer to put her thermometer _____ the car, and I get the
$~~~~~~$**16**

veterinarian to come out and be a witness. It's 60 degrees. "I am not here to arrest

you. I am here to educate you. And _____ that end, I inform you that you also
$~~~~~~$**17**

may not let your dogs out _____ your own fenced yard _____ more time
  18   19
than it takes for them to relieve themselves unless they have access _____ an
                                                                      20
approved insulated shelter _____ bedding and a flap _____ the weather."
                            21   22
"My arctic sled dog and my robust Labrador retriever can't go out and romp

_____ my own property unless I build them a bungalow? Tell me that rule
  23

again." She tells me again! "Tell me one more time." She tells me one more time.

"OK, I have to talk _____ your supervisor."
                     24

The officer pulls out her cell phone. _____ a few minutes, the supervisor
                                         25

pulls up. Now it turned into a scene _____ Schindler's List[2]. The big guy
                                       26

_____ the black uniform, happy as a bird, backs up the insanity the other
  27

officer said. Also, he is detaining us. He's _____ a good mood, telling us
                                              28

anecdotes _____ his thrilling career as an animal welfare officer.
           29

"I'll just tell you this story, and then I'll let you go," he says. "You know, when

you are wearing that uniform and that badge, things you say have a different

weight," I tell him. "Right. I'll just tell you this story, and then I'll let you go." I

finally got away _____ the guy _____ telling him I thought he was doing
                  30   31

a great job protecting animals and educating the public.

I downloaded Section 353-B _____ Article 26 when I got home. Needless
                             32

to say, it bore no resemblance to the stuff the two animal cops had been telling me.

The whole experience left me craving closure. See, in Chicago, when you used to

have this kind of encounter _____ a police officer, it was supposed to end
                             33

_____ money changing hands. I hate amateurs.
  34

---

[2] *Schindler's List*: movie directed by Steven Spielberg in which Jewish prisoners are
saved from death during World War II

A. READING FOR THE MAIN IDEA

Read the editorial. Check the statement that best summarizes the author's main idea.

❑ 1. If you respect speed limits, you could get into trouble.

❑ 2. More people should slow down and respect the speed limits.

❑ 3. The speed limits should be posted more consistently so that drivers always know what the speed limits are.

Unsafe at Any Speed
by Marek Fuchs . . . .

Empty midsummer would seem a not-too-daring time for an experiment behind the wheel, so I decided to try spending an entire week on the roads of Westchester—backcountry to highway—without going a single mile over the speed limit, no matter how slow that was.

This may not appear much of a challenge. But just knowing I can make an engine rev and go wherever I want on the double-charge always does my otherwise mild-mannered suburban soul some good. Trade that constant possibility of **illicit** behavior for a week of strict **obedience**, and the results would be anybody's guess.

Sunday
It was the official day of rest, which means I was up at 6 to play my weekly basketball game in Irvington. I pulled out of my driveway, only to realize that there was no speed limit sign—anywhere. A call to the village police revealed that the default speed limit in our village (the fastest you can go in Hastings if no sign marks the area) is 25 miles an hour.

Fair enough. If you went much faster, it would be dangerous entering the traffic stream on Route 9. But it was just after dawn on Sunday; hardly anybody was even on Route 9. My law-abiding puttering down the road at the **posted** limit of 30 did not **engender road rage**, or even what came to be the common reaction: the parade of cars nipping at my heels, at times appearing in the rearview mirror the size of the Seventh Infantry Division, every fifth vehicle or so

flashing a light as its driver tried to pull into the passing lane.

Another discovery on Route 9 that would **set the tone** for the week: I had to remain self-consciously aware of the speed limit in order not to **creep** higher. The limit—there and almost everywhere else— seemed to be set unrealistically low, turning obedience into a concentrated chore.

Tuesday
In the fast lane on the Saw Mill River Parkway while returning from a dinner in Pleasantville, I was a rolling **provocation**. Three dozen cars romped past me on the right before I hit my exit at Hastings, more than 10 miles south. As **poky** a pace as I was setting at 55, things turned worse just past the county police station, where the posted speed limit dropped to 50. I tapped the brakes, earning a honk and prompting my son—who was by now getting used to the gravitational drag—to pipe up, "What did you do to them, Daddy?"

Friday
I woke up ready to troll for reactions, mannerly and otherwise, during rush hour. It turned out that the Thruway was the wrong place to start: too much traffic even to make it to the speed limit.

Eventually congestion eased up; I took I-684, the Saw Mill and the Sprain, and a spin both ways on the Cross County, all the while trying my best to keep count of cars that passed.

It was a stampede[3]. What does it say about society that a man trying to obey the law is treated like an obstacle and an outcast? I decided to interrupt my experiment to find out just why the speed limit is the most disobeyed law on the books. The National Motorists Association in Waunakee, Wis., seemed a good place to start. It was created in 1982 to fight the 55-mile-an-hour speed limit. The 55-mile-an-hour speed limit was put into effect in 1974.

Eric Skrum, a spokesman, explained that drivers primarily set their pace relative to one another. "Emotion plays a bigger role than traffic engineers," he said. Over time, he added, this habit **undermines** confidence in the law.

Mr. Skrum does not advocate turning anything with a straightaway into a devil's playground; far from it. But he did note that after a generation, the federal government finally acknowledged the **irrelevance** of the 55 limit by lifting it.

He also mentioned the open secret of speed limits: They are purposely set low so that local governments always have the option of raising money the old-fashioned way, by ticketing.

I told him of my driving experiment and was promptly **reprimanded**.

"By doing that, you were the most dangerous one on the road," he said.

It was the best I had felt all week. ∎

---

[3]*stampede*: sudden flight

Originally published in *The New York Times*, July 24, 2005. Copyright © 2005 by the New York Times Company. Reprinted by permission.

B. READING FOR DETAILS

Read the questions and circle the best answer. Compare your answers with those of another student. Refer to the editorial to justify your answers.

1. How does author Marek Fuchs conduct his driving experiment?
   a. by waiting until the summer was over
   b. by speeding down Westchester highways
   c. by driving the speed limit on all roads

2. How does the author usually drive?
   a. He drives over the speed limit.
   b. He drives the speed limit.
   c. He sometimes drives the speed limit and sometimes over the speed limit.

3. Why does the author drive 25 miles an hour on Sunday?
   a. because it was the speed limit for an area with no signs
   b. because a police officer told him to slow down
   c. because it's too dangerous to drive any faster in Hastings

4. Which of the following describes the author's driving experience on Route 9?
   a. It did not engender road rage.
   b. Cars nipped at the heels of the driver.
   c. Drivers flashed their lights at him.

5. What does the author realize about himself as a driver on Route 9?
   a. He was responsible for showing others how to drive.
   b. He was a self-conscious driver.
   c. Driving the speed limit was very difficult and required effort.

6. On which highway is it impossible for cars to pass him?
   a. the Thruway
   b. I-684
   c. the Cross County

7. What happened in 1982?
   a. The National Motorists Association was formed.
   b. The 55-mile-an-hour speed limit was started.
   c. The 1974 speed limit was changed.

8. What does Eric Skrum think about the 55-mile-an-hour speed limit?
   a. He thinks drivers should set their pace to it.
   b. He thinks traffic engineers did a good job setting it.
   c. He thinks it doesn't make sense.

9. Why are speed limits purposely set low?
   a. to raise money by ticketing
   b. to reprimand slow drivers
   c. to prevent danger

C. WORD SEARCH

Look at the boldfaced words in the editorial. Try to determine their meaning from the context. Write the correct word or phrase from the box next to its definition.

creep	irrelevance	posted	road rage
engender	obedience	provocation	set the tone
illicit	poky	reprimanded	undermines

1. _____ : gradually makes something less strong or effective

2. _____ : violence and angry behavior by drivers toward other drivers

3. _____ : not allowed by laws or rules

4. _____ : doing things very slowly, especially in a way that is annoying

5. _____ : told that a behavior is wrong

6. _____: doing what a law or rule says you must do

7. _____: put up as a public notice

8. _____: an action or event that makes or is intended to make someone angry

9. _____: lack of importance in a particular situation

10. _____: move in a quiet, careful way

11. _____: do something in a particular way which then continues for a long time

12. _____: cause; stimulate

V. SYNTHESIZING TWO PIECES

A. DISTINGUISHING OPINIONS

Work in pairs. Go back to the commentary and editorial. Each story represents a law, either one that exists and is enforced (but maybe should not be) or one that exists but is not enforced (but maybe should be). Fill in the information for each of the following themes. The first one has been done for you.

THEMES	PINKWATER (OPINION 1)	FUCHS (OPINION 2)
Law on the books	You cannot leave a dog in a car because it's not an appropriate shelter.	
Person / people respecting, concerned with, or enforcing the law		
Person / people breaking the law		
Irony of law enforcement		

B. GIVING YOUR OPINION

Work in groups. Look at the information in the chart on page 11. Consider what happened in each story as you answer the following questions:

1. Which law(s), if any, should remain on the books?

2. Who do you support more in these two stories: the law abider, the law breaker, or the law enforcer? Why?

C. VOCABULARY REINFORCEMENT: Vocabulary / Concept Grid

Work in groups. Discuss the relationship of the vocabulary to the concepts at the top of the chart.

Put a plus (+) in the box if there is a positive relationship between the vocabulary and the concept (one causes the other, one is an example of the other, one supports the other).

Put a minus (–) in the box if there is a negative relationship between them (one contradicts the other, one is not an example of the other, one does not support the other).

Put a question mark (?) in the box if your group is unsure of the relationship or cannot agree. The first one has been done for you.

"Cops" is . . .
- *positively related (+) to "Enforcing the Law" because cops are law enforcement officers*
- *positively related (+) to "Following the Law" because their job is to be sure that people do it*
- *negatively related (–) to "Breaking the Law" because this contradicts their role as law enforcers*

	ENFORCING THE LAW	FOLLOWING THE LAW	BREAKING THE LAW
cops	+	–	–
detain			
fine			
humane law enforcement officer			
illicit			

	ENFORCING THE LAW	FOLLOWING THE LAW	BREAKING THE LAW
obedience			
posted			
provocation			
reprimanded			
road rage			
stipulates			
subject to			
undermines			
violation			

A. CASE STUDY: Locking a Car

The following reading presents a true case that raises the issue of how laws should be interpreted and whether or not they should be enforced.

Work in small groups. Study the case. Discuss the implications of Susan Guita Silverstein's case. Who was wrong in this case? How should law enforcement have responded? What legal action should be taken? Present your conclusions to the rest of the class.

On a hot summer day, at 1:03 P.M., a 911 call was made from a parking lot in Stamford, Connecticut. A frantic woman, Susan Guita Silverstein, had mistakenly locked her two-year-old son in her car, and it was 88 degrees outside. Recordings of the phone call indicate that she requested that police be sent to watch her child so that she could go home and get another key. Her home was only 1½ miles away, about two minutes away from the parking lot. The person who handled the 911 call told her the fire department would respond.

When the fire department arrived on the scene, they tried, unsuccessfully, to unlock the car. Finally, they said they would have to break the window to rescue the child. Silverstein insisted that she would go home to get a spare key and stated that she did not want them to break the window. Finally, they told her that if she left the scene, they were going to have her arrested. Silverstein found a friend in the parking lot whose car she borrowed to drive home.

(continued)

Upon her return with the key, she saw that her car window had been smashed and her child was being removed from her car, unconscious. She started screaming, "Where's my baby?" and tried to take him. The child was immediately put into an air-conditioned police car and then taken to the hospital in an ambulance. Silverstein was then handcuffed, placed under arrest, and put into the back of a police car. At the hospital, the child was treated and then released. The mother was charged with first-degree reckless endangerment and risk of injury to a minor.

Many people were extremely angry when they heard about this story in the newspapers. In fact, the story gained national attention. The child had been in the car with no ventilation for about 20 minutes. The inside of a closed car in 88-degree temperatures can reach more than 100 degrees in less than five minutes. Many people were shocked that a woman would worry more about the damage to her car than saving her child's life.

Silverstein's husband issued a statement the next day explaining his wife's behavior, saying that she had feared that the shattered glass would injure her child and that she had had no concerns about the car. In fact, when investigators checked the rear passenger compartment of Silverstein's car, they did find broken glass where the child's seat had been placed. Silverstein's lawyer said that it was outrageous that Silverstein's reputation was being destroyed by the media and that his client "was wrongfully restrained, falsely imprisoned, civilly assaulted and battered, and deprived of her rights under the Constitution." He asked for the charges against Silverstein to be dropped.

B. DISCUSSION QUESTIONS

Work in groups. Discuss your answers to the questions.

1. Have you ever heard of someone being arrested for a law that they had broken but did not realize existed? What happened? Tell the story.

2. Discuss laws that you know exist but that law enforcement "turns a blind eye to." Give examples of laws that people know do not need to be followed or will generally not be enforced by the authorities.

3. When people travel to other countries, they are often surprised by some of the laws. Discuss your experience with or knowledge about laws in different countries. Which do you consider to be good ones, ones that your country should adopt? Which do you consider to be silly or unreasonable?

A. GRAMMAR: Use of the Simple Present for Narrative Style in the Past

Notice   Notice the tense that is used by commentator Daniel Pinkwater to tell his story. Why has he chosen to use this tense to talk about something that happened in the past? Where does Pinkwater make tense shifts in his story?

Explanation   The simple present is commonly used when we talk about literature or film. Because fictional events exist outside of reality, writers often use the present tense to describe them. We also use the present tense to narrate past events when we want to bring our listeners more into the story. By using the present tense, the listener becomes part of the story. Listeners hear the story as if they are there when it is happening. Writers and speakers can choose between telling a story in the present tense or past tense. What they should *not* do is switch tenses in the middle of their story. A common error made by students is to shift tenses while telling a story. Writers must choose to tell their stories in the present or past tense. They cannot shift tenses within the story.

Exercise 1: Tense Shifts

Identify the tense shifts in Pinkwater's story. Where is the tense shift appropriate? Where is it not recommended?

Exercise 2: Transformation

Go back to Opinion 2: Reading. Reread the sections "Sunday," "Tuesday," and "Friday." The author tells his story in the past tense. Rewrite these sections in the present tense to bring the reader closer to the story.

Once you have finished writing these excerpts in the present tense, compare your changes with those of a partner. Discuss the effect that the switch makes on the story. Which do you prefer and why?

Exercise 3: Tense Shift Error Correction

Read the excerpts. Identify the tense shift in each piece. Change verbs so that there is no longer a tense shift.

1. So Jill and I decide to duck into Antonella's for a cappuccino after taking our dogs to the vet nearby. We leave the dogs in the car. The dashboard temperature thing indicated that it was 45 degrees, and we had left the sunroof open.

2. I get the officer to put her thermometer in the car, and I get the veterinarian to come out and be a witness. It was 60 degrees.

3. It was just past midnight as I was speeding home. Looking in my rearview mirror, I suddenly notice a car with a flashing red light following me. I pull over, knowing I was going to get a ticket.

4. The sign in the public park says all dogs must be on a leash. But this is my dog's only chance to run free and exercise, so I took off my dog's leash and let him run, knowing very well that I could receive a fine if anybody came along.

5. The traffic light is turning red, so I stop. Any car running a red light is breaking the law, but two cars behind me swerved around my car and ran the red light. As usual, no police officer was to be seen to catch them.

6. Knowing that the woman was probably an undocumented worker, Mrs. Dobbs hired Anna to clean her house. Anna agreed to come twice a week. She comes on her first day, and Mrs. Dobbs pays her in cash.

B. WRITING STYLE: Narration

Notice Notice the writing style of Pinkwater. Without telling us directly, he gets us to think about the absurdity of certain laws and law enforcement. How does he do this?

Explanation Most brief narrative essays focus on a single experience that changed the writer's outlook on something. This is the case for Pinkwater's commentary. Through a personal account of his experience with a humane law enforcement officer and her supervisor, Pinkwater describes the sometimes absurd nature of enforcing the law. He narrates his own story and, through his story, prompts the reader to think about this issue.

In essay writing, the purpose of narration is to inform, support a thesis, and help the essay arrive at its conclusion. A well-told story is hard to forget, which is why narration is especially effective for communicating an idea.

Effective narration has the following characteristics:

1. **A consistent point of view:** Narration should be delivered from the same point of view throughout the story. The most common points of view are the first person ("I"), in which the reader experiences an event through the writer's eyes and ears, and third person ("he"/"she"), in which the writer is not a participant in the action being described. The first person is more subjective; the third person is more objective.

2. **A chronological organization:** There should be a clear beginning, middle, and end to a story. Effective narration proceeds chronologically because time order helps establish what happened and when. Narration should show a clear past, present, and future.

3. **A clear context:** Readers / listeners should know what, to whom, where, when, why, and how things happened.

4. **Effective details:** If details are well chosen, they will help the reader / listener envision the situation being described. Details can provide enough information to help set the scene, but there should not be so many details that the reader / listener becomes confused or overwhelmed.

5. **Quotations:** An effective narration often uses the exact words of others. By using quoted speech in a story, the story comes alive. The reader / listener can "hear" a person talking in the story.

6. **A thesis:** There should be clear idea that provokes thought or discussion about why the author wrote the narration. In other words, there should be a point to the story.

Exercise

Work in pairs. One student looks at Opinion 1 (Pinkwater's commentary), and the other student looks at Opinion 2 (Fuch's editorial). Using the points listed above for effective narration, analyze one of the two narrations. Take notes to answer the following questions. Then present your analysis to your partner. Discuss both analyses with the class.

1. From what point of view does the commentator / writer tell his story? Is

   this point of view consistent? _____

   _____

2. Briefly describe the chronology of the narration:

   Beginning: _____

   Middle: _____

   End: _____

3. Briefly describe the context that the commentator / writer has set for his narration.

What? _____

To whom? _____

Where? _____

When? _____

How? _____

4. List some of the effective details the commentator / writer uses in his

narration. _____

_____

5. Does the commentator / writer use any quotations to enhance his narration? If so, list some examples. _____

_____

_____

6. Although the commentator / writer does not state his thesis directly, he

does present a clear idea. What is the point in the story? _____

_____

_____

C. ESSAY QUESTIONS

Write an essay on one of the topics. Use ideas, vocabulary, grammar, and writing styles you have learned from this unit. Be sure to include an introduction, a body with at least three paragraphs, and a conclusion.

1. Write a narrative essay. Tell a story about a time when you broke the law without even realizing it or broke a law because it seemed irrelevant to you. Or tell a story about a time when you followed the law and felt silly doing so because no one else was following it.

2. In your opinion, which laws on the books are irrelevant? Which laws on the books are important but not enforced? Write an essay in which you describe the laws that do not work in your society. Describe those that are irrelevant to today's world and those that are not enforced but should be.

Better Dead Than Coed?

REAL EDUCATION

MR. PUNCH is of opinion that a polite and easy bearing towards the opposite sex (tempered, of course, with propriety and discretion) cannot be inculcated at too early an age. He therefore recommends that whenever an Institute for Young Ladies happens to meet an Academy for Young Gentlemen, they should be formally introduced to each other, and allowed to take their walks abroad in company.

http://www.cartoonstock.com

I. ANTICIPATING THE ISSUE

Discuss your answers to the questions.

1. Look at the title. Look at the cartoon. What do you think the issue of this unit will be?

2. What is the message or humor of the cartoon?

3. What do you know about the effects of coeducation on students? What do you know about single-sex schooling?

Read the text.

When you stop and think about your high school or college **alma mater**, do you think your experiences were more positive or negative? Do your feelings of success or failure in that school have anything to do with whether your school was single-sex or coed? More and more Americans are **electing** to send their children to single-sex schools because they feel that both boys and girls **blossom** when they study in the company of students of the same sex. They tend to achieve more.

For years, only parents who could afford to send their children to private schools, or who had strong religious or cultural reasons, chose single-sex education for their children. For example, Catholic families often sent their children to **parochial schools**. Since U.S. public schools are, by law, coeducational and free, single-sex schooling was **out of reach** for most American families. Today, though, public schools are experimenting with the idea of separating the sexes. However, because public schools are not allowed to discriminate on the basis of sex, they have been denied federal support.

Girls may be the ones who benefit most from single-sex schooling. Studies have shown that many girls get **shortchanged** in coed classrooms because teachers sometimes pay more attention to boys. Girls' positive, **exuberant** attitude toward their studies tends to disappear as they begin to feel less successful. They start to watch their male peers outperform them in math and science. As boys begin to gain confidence, girls start to lose confidence. Moreover, adolescence is such a **fragile** time for girls. Some girls become depressed, develop an addiction, or suffer from an obsession with weight.

In the early 1990s, the American Association of University Women (AAUW) concluded that being in single-sex classes could raise a girl's **self-esteem**. Schools across the country began creating single-sex classrooms and single-sex schools. But in a later report, that same organization could no longer support the claim that girls performed better without boys in the classroom. In addition, many critics claim that all-female schools may actually be detrimental to a girl's education because they "reinforce regressive notions of sex differences."

The **renewed** interest in single-sex schooling has **fostered** a controversy among Americans. Those who give it full **endorsement** believe girls need an all-female environment to take risks and find their own voices, proclaiming that they're "better dead than coed." Those who question the validity of single-sex schooling wonder whether students' lack of achievement **warrants** returning to an educational system that divides the sexes. They believe there is no such thing as separate but equal.

A. VOCABULARY

Read the sentences. Circle the letter of the word or phrase that is closest in meaning to the boldfaced words. If necessary, use a dictionary.

1. When you stop and think about your high school or college **alma mater**, were your experiences more positive or negative?
   a. school one has attended briefly
   b. school one has applied to
   c. school one has graduated from

2. More and more Americans are **electing** to send their children to single-sex schools because they feel that both boys and girls blossom when they study in the company of students of the same sex.
   a. hesitating
   b. choosing
   c. neglecting

3. More and more Americans are electing to send their children to single-sex schools because they feel both boys and girls **blossom** when they study in the company of students of the same sex. They tend to achieve more.
   a. compete
   b. interact
   c. develop

4. For example, Catholic families often sent their children to **parochial schools**.
   a. integrated schools
   b. schools related to church
   c. schools for boys

5. Since U.S. public schools are, by law, coeducational and free, single-sex schooling was **out of reach** for most American families.
   a. inaccessible
   b. illegal
   c. abnormal

6. Studies have shown that many girls get **shortchanged** in coed classrooms because teachers sometimes pay more attention to boys.
   a. laughed at
   b. hurt
   c. cheated

7. Girls' positive, **exuberant** attitude toward their studies tends to disappear as they begin to feel less successful.
   a. serious
   b. powerful
   c. enthusiastic

8. Moreover, adolescence is such a **fragile** time for girls. As they experience adolescent changes, some girls become depressed, develop an addiction, or suffer from an obsession with weight.
   a. broken
   b. delicate
   c. demanding

9. In the early 1990s, the American Association of University Women (AAUW) concluded that being in single-sex classes could raise a girl's **self-esteem**.
   a. intelligence
   b. confidence
   c. awareness

10. The **renewed** interest in single-sex schooling has fostered a controversy among Americans.
    a. brought back again
    b. remembered
    c. repeated

11. The renewed interest in single-sex schooling has **fostered** a controversy among Americans.
    a. nurtured
    b. discouraged
    c. delayed

12. Those who give it full **endorsement** believe girls need an all-female environment to take risks and find their own voices.
    a. approval
    b. criticism
    c. understanding

13. Those who question the validity of single-sex schooling wonder whether students' lack of achievement **warrants** returning to an educational system that divides the sexes.
    a. equals
    b. requires
    c. justifies

B. SUMMARIZING THE ISSUE

Work with another student. Write a five-sentence summary of the issue.

_____

_____

_____

_____

_____

C. VALUES CLARIFICATION

Work in small groups. Based on your own educational experiences, check whether you agree or disagree with the following points. Discuss your answers.

	AGREE	DISAGREE
Girls blossom when they study in all-girls schools.		
Boys blossom when they study in all-boys schools.		
Girls are more exuberant about school before adolescence.		
The separation of the sexes reinforces ideas about sex differences.		
Separate education can never mean equal education.		

III. OPINION 1: LISTENING

A. LISTENING FOR THE MAIN IDEAS

Read the questions. Then listen to the commentary and answer the questions.

1. What conclusion did the AAUW eventually come to?

   _____

2. According to the commentator, how are girls different from boys?

   _____

3. Does the commentator agree or disagree with the conclusions of the report? Give two reasons to support your answer.

   _____

   _____

B. LISTENING FOR DETAILS

Listen to the commentary again. Distinguish the ideas expressed by the commentator, Katharine Ferguson, from those presented by others. Check each statement that supports Ferguson's opinion.

❏ 1. American girls are being shortchanged in classrooms.

❏ 2. Single-sex schooling is not the solution for girls' classroom problems.

❏ 3. The AAUW study may not have asked the right questions.

❏ 4. The experiments in all-girls schooling should continue.

❏ 5. Girls' test scores do not warrant endorsement of single-sex classrooms.

❏ 6. Because self-esteem is difficult to measure, Carol Gilligan's work cannot support single-sex schooling.

❏ 7. Girls cannot perform as well as boys in math and science.

❏ 8. All-girls schools are reserved for rich families.

❏ 9. Public schools cannot afford girls-only schools—not all girls need them.

❏ 10. Girls need to take more intellectual risks.

C. TEXT COMPLETION AND DISCRETE LISTENING

Read the commentary. Fill in the missing words. Then listen again to check your answers. If your answers differ from the commentary, ask your teacher if they are acceptable alternatives.

Introduction

Six years ago, the American Association of University Women issued a major report: American girls were being _____ in classrooms. Last week, the same organization said, based on _____ achievement levels of students, it could not _____ single-sex education as the solution to the problems girls face in the American education system. Commentator Katharine Ferguson wonders if the study asked the right questions.

Commentary

It's a shame that the AAUW took a _____ at single-sex classrooms in schools. Their latest report will hurt most those handful of experiments in public school systems.

The university women concluded that overall test scores for the girls involved have not risen _____ 5 enough to _____ 6 endorsement of single-sex classrooms. The organization is missing the point.

Harvard researcher Carol Gilligan has done important work on _____ 7 girls. She's let us see how different they are from boys their age—their learning styles, their value systems, the cultural messages they _____ 8 . It is, she's found, a fragile time for girls, who often, as early as ten or eleven, begin to lose the exuberant _____ 9 we often see in little girls.

An all-girls school can help _____ 10 that loss of self-confidence, instead _____ 11 the self-esteem that can carry a young girl through high school, into college, and _____ 12 . That kind of learning is more difficult to measure.

At my _____ 13 _____ 14 , a single-sex boarding school in the Washington, D.C., suburbs, many girls are _____ 15 to take additional classes in math and science. More girls are enrolled in advanced _____ 16 physics and chemistry than ever before, and many of them continue to study math and science in college.

The National Coalition of Girls Schools reports that those attending all-girls schools test higher than the national average. There's a _____ 17 interest in an all-girls education. Applications are _____ 18 up. And don't think these are all from rich families. There are many families choosing to send a child to a _____ 19 all-girls secondary school, even when it means _____ 20 a private college education. They've decided the time to invest in their daughter's education is in secondary school, when it can _____ 21 the most difference.

For the most part, all-girls schools have only been available to those who could afford to pay private and _____ school tuitions, something which is out of reach for most Americans. That's why the _____ with all-girl classrooms within public school systems are so important. All girls may not need the experience of a female-only education, but I believe some girls will always do better, will _____, away from boys in a setting where they feel safe to take intellectual risks, to speak out in class, to make a mistake and not be embarrassed.

So, let's give the experiments a little more time and study. They're _____ it. _____ our girls.

22   23   24   25   26

IV. OPINION 2: READING

A. READING FOR THE MAIN IDEAS

Read the article on pages 27–28. Answer the questions with complete sentences.

1. How did the pattern of education change for women from the 1800s to the 1900s?

   _____

2. In which area of education is coeducation being challenged the most?

   _____

3. What is the main problem with studies that have looked at the success of women in single-sex schooling, according to essayist Wendy Kaminer?

   _____

4. Why is Kaminer opposed to a return to single-sex schooling?

   _____

The Trouble with Single-Sex Schools

by Wendy Kaminer

American women won the opportunity to be educated nearly a hundred years before they won the right to vote, not coincidentally. In the beginning, women were educated for the sake of family and society: The new republic needed educated mothers to produce reasonable, responsible male citizens. But although the first all-female academies, founded in the early 1800s, reflected a commitment to traditional gender roles, which reserved the public sphere for men, they reinforced a nascent view of women as potentially reasonable human beings—**endowed** with the attributes of citizenship.

Education also contributed to women's restlessness and impatience with domesticity. It may or may not have produced better mothers, but it did seem to produce fewer mothers. Young female secondary-school graduates of the mid-1800s tended to marry later than their uneducated peers or not at all. "Our failures only marry," the president of Bryn Mawr, M. Carey Thomas, famously remarked in the early 1900s.

The first generations of educated women were products of single-sex secondary and undergraduate schools, with few exceptions . . . . Such schools were essential to the nineteenth-century women's movement. They not only inspired activism in women and prepared them to work outside the home but also created wage-earning work, as school teaching became one of few respectable professional options for unmarried females.

Still, single-sex education was not exactly a choice; it was a cultural **mandate** at a time when sexual segregation was considered only natural. Early feminists hoped eventually to integrate men's schools as well as voting booths, and equal educational opportunities proved much easier to obtain than equal electoral rights. By the turn of the century more girls than boys were graduating from high school and coeducation was becoming the norm. In 1910, out of the nation's 1,083 colleges, 27 percent were exclusively for men, 15 percent exclusively for women, and the remaining 58 percent coed . . . .

[Today,] having gained entry to virtually all the nation's public and private universities (and military academies), many women are questioning the benefits of coeducation at every level, but especially in secondary schools. According to popular feminist wisdom, coed schools are detrimental to the self-esteem of girls; they discourage rather than inspire girls' achievement, particularly in math and science. . . . All-girls elementary and secondary schools are in the midst of a "renaissance," according to Whitney Ransome, the director of the National Coalition of Girls' Schools. Since the early 1990s, applications have increased by 21 percent and four new all-girls secondary schools have been established . . . .

Conservatives, who are generally unsympathetic to arguments about self-esteem, dismissing them as an expression of liberal "victimism," find themselves extolling the virtues of a nurturing, supportive environment that builds girls' confidence and capacity to lead. In their defense of girls' schools, however, they rely primarily on a traditional belief that maintaining separate schools for males and females is only natural, considering presumed differences in their developmental needs and learning styles . . . .

In addition to assumptions about female learning and relational styles, **proponents** of all-girls schools rely on social science to support the claim that segregation by sex fosters achievement in girls. "Studies show . . ." is the usual lead-in to any defense of single-sex education. In fact studies do not show that girls **fare** better in single-sex schools. "There does not seem to be research support for this perspective," the sociologist Cynthia Epstein politely observes. Epstein, the author of *Deceptive Distinctions: Sex, Gender, and the Social Order* (1988), adds that there is no **consensus** among psychologists as to the existence of psychological or cognitive differences between the sexes and that the evidence for the need for single-sex education and the justice of single-sex schools is highly **equivocal** . . . .

What then is the basis for the claim that "studies show" the advantages of all-female schools? Perhaps the most frequently cited studies were conducted by M. Elizabeth Tidball, who reviewed the educational backgrounds of female achievers. In her first widely cited study, published in 1973, Tidball examined a random sample of women included in *Who's Who* and found that disproportionate numbers were graduates of women's colleges. In **subsequent** studies Tidball found that women's colleges

(continued)

produced more than their share of graduates who went on to medical school or received doctorates in the natural or life sciences.

What do these studies tell us about the relationship between single-sex education and achievement? Virtually nothing. Tidball made the common mistake of confusing **correlation** with **causation**. As Faye Crosby, a professor of psychology at Smith College, and other critics have observed, Tidball did not control for characteristics of women's colleges, apart from sexual homogeneity, that might well account for the success of their graduates. She did not allow for the socioeconomic privileges shared by many graduates of elite women's colleges or for the selectivity of the schools.

Tidball's 1973 study focuses on women who graduated from women's colleges in the years before elite men's colleges were integrated. . . . Students at these schools were self-selected for success, like their male counterparts in the Ivy League. They also tended to be well connected; many may have owed their success to the males present in their families more than to the absence of males from their classes. . . . There are no definitive comparative data on the benefits of single-sex colleges for women. "Data are slim," Crosby writes, "but they indicate that coeducational schools are as likely to produce women scientists as are women's colleges."

Crosby's assertion challenges conventional wisdom about the risks of coeducation, which is becoming increasingly fashionable in secondary schools. A recent, widely cited study commissioned by the American Association of University Women (prepared by the Wellesley College Center for Research on Women) decries the current system. . . . "Girls and boys enter school roughly equal in measured ability. Twelve years later, girls have fallen behind their male classmates in key areas such as higher-level mathematics and measures of self-esteem . . . "

Are schools "shortchanging girls"? Reading the entire AAUW report, it's hard to say. "There is considerable evidence that girls earn higher grades than boys throughout their school careers," the report acknowledges. And the sexes seem to be approaching **parity** in skills. Recent research indicates that "sex differences in verbal abilities have decreased markedly . . . [and] differences in mathematics achievement are small and declining . . . "

The AAUW study suggests that high school girls have less self-esteem than boys and that the self-esteem of girls declines dramatically after puberty.

How did the researchers measure self-esteem? They counted the number of elementary school and high school students who reported being "happy the way I am." Sixty-nine percent of elementary school boys and 60 percent of elementary school girls declared that they were indeed happy with themselves. But among high school students, 46 percent of boys were "happy the way I am" and a mere 29 percent of girls.

It's impossible to know what this survey means. Maybe it is evidence that girls have low self-esteem, as the AAUW report suggests. Or maybe it demonstrates that girls are less complacent and more ambitious than boys, and more likely to hold themselves to high standards of performance. Maybe boys are **in a rut**. Maybe not. By itself, "Are you happy with yourself?" is a useless survey question, because interpretations of the answer are hopelessly subjective.

What additional evidence is there to support the common assumption that girls are more likely to suffer a drop in self-esteem as they enter their teens? The AAUW report cites recent work, by Carol Gilligan, Lyn Mikel Brown, and Annie Rogers, documenting "silencing of girls" in junior high and high school. But even if their findings on a loss of confidence in girls are accurate, these tell us very little about sexism or sex difference, because they offer no comparable study of boys. Maybe a loss of self-esteem is a function of adolescence, not of sex. Maybe boys are silenced too, metaphorically if not in fact. Maybe they make noise to drown out their fears. Maybe not. . . .

Forty years ago the Supreme Court struck down racial segregation, relying in part on **empirical** evidence that racially separate schools were inherently unequal. We ought not to embrace a standard of separate but equal schools for males and females without equivalent empirical evidence that they are needed and likely to make progress toward equality. A hundred and fifty years ago the drive to establish separate but equal schools for men and women was necessitated by the separation of the sexes in social and political life. A hundred and fifty years ago, when women were excluded from men's academies, women's academies did indeed represent affirmative action[1]. Today a return to separate single-sex schools may hasten the revival of separate gender roles. Only as the sexes have become less separate have women become more free. ∎

From *The Atlantic Monthly*, April 1998. © 1998 Wendy Kaminer. Reprinted by permission.

[1]*affirmative action:* policies to advance minorities

B. READING FOR DETAILS

Read the questions and circle the best answer. Compare your answers with those of another student. Refer to the article to justify your answers.

1. Why were women first educated in American society?
   a. to become knowledgeable enough to vote
   b. to develop new professions for society
   c. to produce educated sons

2. Education produced _____ mothers.
   a. better
   b. fewer
   c. unmarried

3. Which result is *not* attributed to early single-sex secondary and undergraduate schools?
   a. They promoted women to the middle class.
   b. They inspired activism.
   c. They created new jobs.

4. By the early 1900s, _____.
   a. coeducation was a choice
   b. single-sex schooling was a state mandate
   c. more girls than boys were attending college

5. In 1910, _____ colleges were the most common type of college in the United States.
   a. men's
   b. women's
   c. coed

6. Conservatives _____.
   a. do not support single-sex schools
   b. worry that girls have been victimized
   c. believe that men and women should be in separate schools

7. According to the author, studies _____.
   a. show that girls perform better in single-sex schools
   b. show that girls perform better in coed schools
   c. do not show that girls perform better in single-sex schools

8. What was wrong with Tidball's research, according to the author?
   a. She focused on sexual homogeneity in her study.
   b. She did not consider the fact that the schools the women attended were elite schools.
   c. She did not include the Ivy League schools in her study.

9. According to Kaminer, the best predictor of grades is _____.
   a. gender
   b. race
   c. social class

10. The AAUW report tells us that _____.
    a. girls' and boys' grades are quite similar
    b. girls have more skills than boys
    c. sex differences in verbal and math achievement are declining

11. The self-esteem survey shows that _____.
    a. elementary school girls and boys are about equally happy with themselves
    b. boys and girls are as happy with themselves in high school as they are in elementary school
    c. more girls than boys are happy with themselves in high school

12. What is wrong with the self-esteem survey, according to Kaminer?
    a. It asks biased questions.
    b. The results are impossible to interpret.
    c. It is too ambitious.

13. How does Kaminer compare single-sex schooling with racial segregation?
    a. Gender and racial segregation are not the same thing.
    b. They both imply inequality.
    c. They both represent affirmative action.

C. WORD SEARCH

Read the sentences from the article. Choose the word or phrase from the box that is closest in meaning to the boldfaced word. Write your choice below each sentence.

advocates	mutual relationship
born with qualities	open to doubt
causing something to happen	order or command
do	relying on observation and experiment
equality	set in a way of doing things
general agreement	and not likely to change
later	

1. But although the first all-female academies, founded in the early 1800s, reflected a commitment to traditional gender roles, which reserved the public sphere for men, they reinforced a nascent view of women as potentially reasonable human beings—**endowed** with the attributes of citizenship.

_____

2. Still, single-sex education was not exactly a choice; it was a cultural **mandate** at a time when sexual segregation was considered only natural.

_____

3. In addition to assumptions about female learning and relational styles, **proponents** of all-girls schools rely on social science to support the claim that segregation by sex fosters achievement in girls.

_____

4. In fact studies do not show that girls **fare** better in single-sex schools.

_____

5. Epstein adds that there is no **consensus** among psychologists as to the existence of psychological or cognitive differences between the sexes and that the evidence for the need for single-sex education and the justice of single-sex schools is highly equivocal.

_____

6. Epstein adds that there is no consensus among psychologists as to the existence of psychological or cognitive differences between the sexes and that the evidence for the need for single-sex education and the justice of single-sex schools is highly **equivocal**.

_____

7. In **subsequent** studies Tidball found that women's colleges produced more than their share of graduates who went on to medical school or received doctorates in the natural or life sciences.

_____

8. Tidball made the common mistake of confusing **correlation** with causation.

_____

9. Tidball made the common mistake of confusing correlation with **causation**.

_____

10. And the sexes seem to be approaching **parity** in skills. Recent research indicates that "sex differences in verbal abilities have decreased markedly . . . [and] differences in mathematics achievement are small and declining."

_____

11. Or maybe it demonstrates that girls are less complacent and more ambitious than boys, and more likely to hold themselves to high standards of performance. Maybe boys are **in a rut**.

_____

12. Forty years ago the Supreme Court struck down racial segregation, relying in part on **empirical** evidence that racially separate schools were inherently unequal.

_____

V. SYNTHESIZING TWO OPINION PIECES

A. DISTINGUISHING OPINIONS

Work in groups. Review the commentary and the article. Take notes to support the views of commentator Katharine Ferguson and essayist Wendy Kaminer on the following topics.

1. Girls' performance in single-sex schools

   Ferguson: _____   **Kaminer:** _____

   _____   _____

   _____   _____

2. Reference to studies that have looked at gender issues and education

   Ferguson: _____   **Kaminer:** _____

   _____   _____

   _____   _____

3. Socioeconomic status of girls attending all-girls schools

   Ferguson: _____   **Kaminer:** _____

   _____   _____

   _____   _____

4. Girls who study math and science

Ferguson: _____   Kaminer: _____

_____   _____

_____   _____

B. GIVING YOUR OPINION

Which opinions in Part A do you share? What experiences have led you to these opinions? Discuss your ideas with your classmates.

C. VOCABULARY REINFORCEMENT: Word Forms

Work in small groups. Fill in the missing word forms for each vocabulary item in the chart. (An *X* has been placed in the box if there is no related word form.) Use a dictionary if necessary.

NOUNS	VERBS	ADJECTIVES	ADVERBS
	elect		electively
X	foster		X
	X	fragile	X
	X	exuberant	
		renewed	X
endorsement			X
		endowed	X
mandate			X
correlation			correlatively

Complete the sentences with the correct word form from the chart.

1. The drop in self-esteem of young women _____ a new interest among many parents in single-sex schooling.

2. Kaminer finds a _____ between the effects of racial segregation and gender segregation on students.

3. According to Carol Gilligan, the _____ of ten- or eleven-year-old girls is often lost when they enter adolescence.

4. In the late 1800s, single-sex education was _____. Women were not allowed to study in the company of men.

5. The _____ of girls during adolescence may be the key to why they lose their self-esteem and perform poorly in math and science.

6. Parents have shown a _____ interest in sending their girls to single-sex schools, especially at the secondary level.

7. Single-sex schools are no longer _____ by the American Association of University Women.

8. The student had the natural _____ of having a good ear for music.

9. The parents _____ to enroll their daughter in a single-sex school, believing it would protect her from the distractions of boys.

A. CASE STUDY: Dartmouth College Fraternities and Sororities

The following reading presents a true case that raises the issue of whether single-sex or coeducational experiences may be best for students. Study the case.

Dartmouth College, founded in 1769, belongs to the "Ivy League"—a highly selective group of private colleges and universities in the United States. In 1972 Dartmouth went from being an all-male college to a coeducational college. By the 1990s, Dartmouth enrolled roughly equal numbers of male and female students. However, some students and faculty there would say that despite this statistical equality, gender relations on campus are strained.

Blame for the problem has been placed on the college's "Greek" system. This system, which exists at many colleges and universities, is a social system whereby a number of private, single-sex student residences called "fraternities" (for men) or "sororities" (for women) exist on or near campus. Nearly 50 percent of Dartmouth students in their third or fourth years at the college belong to one of the 25 Greek "houses" on campus. New students who want to join must be selected by current house members in order to belong.

For several years officials at the college called for vast reform of or an end to single-sex fraternities and sororities, in part because they maintain that the Greek system promotes a culture of discrimination, including sexism. Officials believe that a change in this residential and social system would help foster "respectful relations between women and men."

An incident that occurred several years ago renewed discussion about the role of the Greek system in perpetuating sexist behavior on campus. This incident involved the publication of a secret fraternity newsletter containing text and photos that were insulting to women. When the newsletter became public, the fraternity was "de-recognized" by the college, meaning that it will no longer function as a fraternity there; the college will take over the house and convert it to another use. After the newsletter incident, 101 Dartmouth professors signed a letter asking for an end to the Greek system. The professors' letter stated disappointment in the results of previous calls for reform: "It was our expectation that finally, after 25 years of coeducation, Dartmouth was ready to take action against institutionalized forms of discrimination and segregation that still dominated student social life, and which we deem so antithetical[2] to the fostering of a truly coeducational academic and residential culture." At a faculty meeting about the Greek system, one English professor remarked that he did not want people to see Dartmouth as a "failed experiment in coeducation." He went on to say that he personally knew two women who chose not to attend Dartmouth because of the prejudices fostered by the Greek system.

Members of fraternities and sororities say that they are not exclusionary because they often include members of different races and sexual orientation. They claim that their fellow residents in the single-sex houses provide friendship and support.

The majority of students at Dartmouth favor reforming the Greek system and approve of the punishments handed down by the college. However, many are concerned about proposals to end the system because they depend on fraternities and sororities to meet their needs for a social life in the small New Hampshire town where the college is located. The houses offer independent social events planned by the students themselves. The alternative would be to have all social activities organized by the college, an idea that would not please most students.

Prepare for a role play. Read the situation and the roles, and follow the procedure.

The Situation

Dartmouth students, alumni[3], and faculty have strong opinions about the administration's proposal to end fraternities and sororities. Under pressure from the faculty, the trustees of the college have called a meeting to discuss the issue. At this meeting, they have asked to hear views of various students on campus.

The Roles

1. **The trustees of Dartmouth College:** You are considering eliminating fraternities and sororities on campus. You worry that the Greek system reinforces and even fosters sexist attitudes among students on campus. Professors have been pressuring you to eliminate the Greek system, claiming that it works against their desire to teach openness and nondiscrimination. Recent fraternity incidents involving discrimination have prompted heated debate on campus. You are interested in hearing students' opinions.

---

[2]*antithetical*: in opposition to
[3]*alumni*: former attendees or graduates

(continued)

2. **Students who have participated in the Greek system:** You represent the nearly 50 percent of third- and fourth-year students as well as many alumni who have experienced belonging to the 25 fraternities and sororities at Dartmouth. You are deeply troubled by the fact that the administration is considering an end to a 160-year-old tradition. Many of your important relationships were formed in the fraternity or sorority that you joined. The single-sex environment helped build your self-esteem and leadership skills. The Greek system provided a social experience and volunteer opportunities, as well as a supportive academic environment that helped you thrive throughout the college years.

3. **Students who have not participated in the Greek system:** You represent the nearly 50 percent of third- and fourth-year students who do not participate in the Greek system. You feel that when the college became coeducational in 1972, it should have abandoned its support for the Greek system as well. You have been disturbed by the recent incident involving the sexist fraternity newsletter. You care deeply about the academic reputation of the college and worry that the Greek system discourages bright women from attending Dartmouth.

The Procedure

1. Form three groups for the three roles.

2. The trustees prepare questions for all students. The students who have participated in the Greek system prepare arguments in favor of preserving the system. The students who have not participated in the system prepare arguments in favor of eliminating the system.

3. The trustees conduct the meeting, asking questions and allowing students to voice their opinions.

4. The trustees meet separately to determine whether they will recommend continuing or ending the Greek system. The decision is presented to the class. ▼

B. DISCUSSION QUESTIONS

Work in groups. Discuss your answers to the questions.

1. Much has been written about the problems of coeducation for girls. But what about boys? How could same-sex schooling also benefit boys? In what situations?

2. The AAUW report cites "gender bias as a major problem at all levels of schooling." Elsewhere, the report states that "girls are plagued by sexual harassment, even at the grade-school level, and neglected by sexist teachers, who pay more attention to boys." How does this description of American schools compare with your own experiences in school? Discuss your perceptions of different cultural attitudes toward the education of girls and boys.

A. GRAMMAR: Noun Clauses

Notice Notice the structure of the underlined phrases in these four sentences taken from the commentary by Katharine Ferguson.

> a. Commentator Katharine Ferguson wonders *if the study asked the right questions*.
> b. She's let us see *how different they are from boys their age*.
> c. The National Coalition of Girls Schools reports *that those attending all-girls schools test higher than the national average*.
> d. That's *why the experiments with all-girls classrooms within public school systems are so important*.

How do these phrases function in the sentences? In what way are they the same or different?

Explanation In all four sentences, the underlined phrases are functioning as nouns; they are called noun clauses. In the first three sentences, the noun clause functions as the object of its sentence. In the fourth sentence, the noun clause is a complement.

A noun clause allows a speaker or writer to describe an idea more fully or to give a noun more emphasis. It can give more information than a single noun.

To introduce a noun clause, question words (such as *how* or *why*) are often used. However, statement word order (subject + verb + object) should be used, even when a distinct question word order exists.

The first three examples above illustrate three categories of noun clauses. Notice the use of noun clauses in the answers to the questions in the box.

Noun Clauses Related to *Yes/No* Questions

if

Did the study ask the right questions?
*Ferguson wonders **if the study asked the right questions**.*

whether

Did the study ask the right questions?
*Ferguson wonders **whether the study asked the right questions**.*

(continued)

Noun Clauses Related to *Wh-* Questions

how

How different are they from boys their age?
*She's let us see **how different they are from boys their age.***

who

Who chooses single-sex schools for their children?
*I don't know **who chooses single-sex schools for their children.***

whose

Whose daughters are attending all-girls schools?
*I don't know **whose daughters are attending all-girls schools.***

which

Which study recommended single-sex schooling?
*I don't recall **which study recommended single-sex schooling.***

why

Why do girls lose their self-esteem during adolescence?
*I'm not sure **why girls lose their self-esteem during adolescence.***

In the next example, notice that the noun clause is in the subject position:

what

What did the AAUW report state?

***What the AAUW report stated** was that overall test scores for girls have not risen enough to warrant endorsement of single-sex classrooms.*

Noun Clauses Used after Reporting Verbs: *report, believe, claim, decide, know, say, think*

*The National Coalition of Girls Schools reports **(that) those attending all-girls schools test higher than the national average.***

Notice that these noun clauses begin with the word *that*. *That* can be dropped in these noun clauses.

Exercise

Rewrite the statements with noun clauses in either the subject or object position. Use information from Wendy Kaminer's article to complete your answers.

1. What contributed to women's restlessness and impatience with domesticity?

   What _____

   _____.

2. How important are the results from the survey?

   It's difficult to judge _____.

3. Who can tell parents more about this issue?

   I know _____.

4. Which school admits only boys?

   We can't remember _____.

5. Has education produced better mothers? It did seem to produce fewer mothers.

   Kaminer questions _____

   but claims _____.

6. Whose opinions are more valuable?

   It's not easy to decide _____.

7. According to popular feminist wisdom, coed schools are detrimental to the self-esteem of girls.

   Popular feminist wisdom believes _____

   _____.

8. Why do disproportionate numbers of women from women's colleges do well?

   In her study, M. Elizabeth Tidball explains _____

   _____.

9. According to the AAUW report, "the educational system is not meeting girls' needs."

   The American Association of University Women reported

   _____

   _____.

10. Are schools shortchanging girls?

    Kaminer wonders _____.

11. How did the researchers measure self-esteem?

    Kaminer asks _____.

12. What does this survey mean?

    It's impossible to know _____.

B. WRITING STYLE: Parallel Structure

Notice Notice the form of the words in boldface in the following examples from Katharine Ferguson's commentary:

> *All girls may not need the experience of a female-only education, but I believe some girls* **will always do better, will blossom,** *away from boys in a setting where they feel safe* **to take intellectual risks, to speak out in class, to make a mistake and not be embarrassed.**

What do you notice about the grammatical forms of the various groups highlighted in the example? What can you say about this style of writing?

Explanation Parallel structure is a construction that expresses a combination of ideas in similar grammatical form. When listing several ideas, it is important to maintain parallel structure.

Most parts of speech can be placed in a parallel construction. In the example above, the first two expressions are both in future verb tenses. The second three expressions are infinitive verb structures.

Exercise

Correct the errors in parallel structure in the underlined parts of the sentences.

1. Many American parents are enrolling their girls in all-girls schools and at the <u>secondary level</u> in order to help their self-esteem.

   _____

   _____

2. Girls are said to succeed more in mathematics, science, and <u>playing sports</u> when they are in an all-girls environment.

   _____

   _____

3. Studies have shown that there are marked differences among girls who study in all-girls schools: an improved self-esteem, a renewed interest in their studies, <u>and they are willing to take risks</u>.

   _____

   _____

4. To separate boys and girls in schools is <u>segregating</u> men and women unequally in our society.

_____

_____

5. When parents choose whether to send their children to a single-sex or coed school, they must consider the school's curriculum, location, and <u>paying the tuition</u>.

_____

_____

C. ESSAY QUESTIONS

Write an essay on one of the numbered topics. Use ideas, vocabulary, and writing techniques from this unit. Try to incorporate the following:

- an introductory paragraph that presents the various sides of the argument and clearly states your thesis

- paragraphs (at least three) that develop your argument with supporting evidence

- a conclusion that reinforces the position you have taken and includes a new idea (a warning, prediction, value judgment) that has not been mentioned before

1. Katharine Ferguson concludes her commentary by saying that we should give the experiments with all-girls classrooms in public school systems more time and study. Do you agree with her? Write an essay in which you express your opinion.

2. Wendy Kaminer concludes her essay by saying, "Only as the sexes have become less separate have women become more free." What is she suggesting in terms of single-sex schooling? Do you agree with her conclusion, based on what you have learned about single-sex schooling? Write an essay in which you express your opinion.

UNIT 3

The Global Child

*"We're so excited. I'm hoping for a Chinese girl, but
Peter's heart is set on a Native American boy."*

I. ANTICIPATING THE ISSUE

Discuss your answers to the questions.

1. Look at the title. Look at the cartoon. What do you think the issue of this unit will be?

2. What is the message or humor of the cartoon?

3. What do you think are the pros and cons of adopting children internationally?

Read the text.

According to UNICEF (United Nations Children's Fund), there are currently 143 million orphans in 93 developing nations. About 135,000 children are adopted inter-country each year. In recent decades, international adoptions have increased dramatically. They nearly tripled from 1990 to 2004. China, for example, sent out over 50,000 children in one decade (1996–2006), largely because of its one-child policy. Yet, this increase in international adoptions has recently taken a downward turn.

Inter-country adoptions have fallen 10 percent in those nations receiving the most children: the United States, Spain, France, Italy, and Canada. Many countries are now reluctant to send children abroad for adoption. There is a concern that these children will suffer without the knowledge of their **indigenous** culture. Moreover, there have been recent charges of corruption in the business of selling babies. Romania and Cambodia have halted international adoptions for this reason. Guatemala, the third-largest source of international adoptions, has also ended its program, as private lawyers, rather than government agencies, were controlling adoptions there. Many people had **taken to** adopting Vietnamese babies, but in 2008, the Vietnamese ended their child-adoption agreement with the United States because of apparent baby-selling and corruption in Vietnam. In one case, a Vietnamese mother felt forced to sell her baby because she couldn't pay her hospital bills. **Weeping** mothers have been pressured to sell their babies by brokers who **dodge** the law by going directly to villages in search of babies to sell. Bulgaria will only **give up** a child for inter-country adoption after the child has already been rejected by three Bulgarian families. Russia put a temporary end to its international adoption program when it discovered reports that 14 Russian children had been killed by their foreign adoptive parents since the 1990s. Americans hoping to adopt Chinese babies have **encountered** a 60 percent reduction in their rate of success as China has changed its criteria for adoption: The Chinese now exclude parents who are single, gay, recently divorced, married less than two years, over 50, overweight, or earning less than $80,000 a year.

Some say that these new criteria are the result of falling birthrates, higher standards of living, higher infertility, and growing national pride in the countries that send children out. Countries such as South Korea, Russia, Kenya, and Brazil now discourage foreign adoptions. The only country where adoptions are growing is Ethiopia, where one celebrity adopted a child. Many who saw the celebrity **strut** through the streets with the baby were critical. However, this celebrity has encouraged other Americans to adopt babies in Africa, making Ethiopia one of the top 10 countries where Americans adopt. Prospective adoptive parents are trying to **figure out** where to find available children. Some are now seeking "special needs" children (those with disabilities) because the wait for these children is significantly shorter and adoption is more certain.

Organizations that oversee foreign adoptions are beginning to strengthen the rules and regulations of international adoption and are encouraging adoptions at home. The Hague Convention on Inter-Country Adoption, which the United States joined in 2008, was designed to make international adoptions safer for the child and both the biological and adoptive parents. More than 70 countries have joined this agreement that attempts to end the international baby trade by establishing licensing requirements for adoption agencies. UNICEF has also taken a position on international adoptions. It **fields** questions related to international adoption, taking the position that orphaned children should remain in their home countries. Thus, international adoptions have been made more difficult. With stricter inter-country regulations, it is **inevitable** that fewer children will be adopted and that some children will spend more time in orphanages. This is **bringing** the orphan problem **full circle** and again leaving a **gaping hole** between the number of children who need loving homes and the number of children who can be legally adopted.

A. VOCABULARY

Match the boldfaced words and phrases in the Background Reading with their definitions below. Write the word or phrase next to its definition.

1. _____ : coming back to how things were at first

2. _____ : walk in a way to impress others

3. _____ : deals with; handles

4. _____ : incapable of being avoided or prevented

5. _____ : natural to a country; native

6. _____ : abandon; release; relinquish

7. _____ : met; ran into

8. _____ : solve the problem of

9. _____ : crying

10. _____ : try to avoid fulfilling duties

11. _____ : developed a habit for; fancied

12. _____ : wide gulf, separation

B. SUMMARIZING THE ISSUE

Work in small groups. Take notes on the developing trends in international adoptions. Summarize the issue.

1. General development of international adoptions: _____

_____

_____

2. Current situation of international adoptions: _____

_____

_____

3. Organizations enforcing new restrictions: _____

_____

_____

4. The issue: _____

_____

C. VALUES CLARIFICATION

Work in small groups. Discuss your answers to the questions.

1. Do you think that it is a good idea to adopt babies from other countries? Why or why not?

2. Do you agree with the concerns that are currently limiting inter-country adoptions? Should they be limited?

III. OPINION 1: LISTENING

A. LISTENING FOR THE MAIN IDEA

Listen to the commentary. Check the statement that best summarizes the commentator's main idea.

❑ 1. It is important to take an adopted child to his or her country of origin so the child can understand his or her heritage.

❑ 2. It's a wonderful thing that a Guatemalan girl can adapt to the American lifestyle and become "American."

❑ 3. A child can be bicultural, of two worlds.

Listen again and answer the questions. Compare your answers with those of another student. Listen again if necessary.

1. Where is Raquel's current home, and where is she going home to?

   _____

2. How old was Raquel when she moved to the States?

   _____

3. What does commentator Marcos McPeek Villatoro hang on the walls to remind his daughter that she's a Guatemalan?

   _____

4. How does Villatoro describe their trip to her home country?

   _____

5. Where does Raquel go that makes her such a Californian?

   _____

6. What happened to Raquel's brothers?

   _____

7. How does Michelle, Raquel's mother, explain the child's adoption?

   _____

8. What had happened to Raquel's old house?

   _____

9. How does Raquel react to seeing her old house?

   _____

10. Why does Raquel spend so much time in bed when she gets home? What is she trying to figure out?

    _____

11. According to Villatoro, is Raquel's home in Guatemala or in California?

    _____

C. TEXT COMPLETION AND DISCRETE LISTENING

Read the commentary. Fill in the missing words. Then listen again to check your answers. If your answers differ from the commentary, ask your teacher if they are acceptable alternatives.

Introduction

Novelist and *Day to Day* contributing writer Marcos McPeek Villatoro took his _____ daughter back to the country where she was born, and
1

where they shared an unforgettable _____.
2

Commentary

I took my daughter home. We had _____ out of Los Angeles at
3

three in the morning. By midnight of the same day, we pulled a rental van through

a hundred miles of _____ and parked in Raquel's hometown of
4

Poptun in the nation of Guatemala.

Raquel is 17. Michelle and I adopted her when she was 12 _____
5

old and we were _____ of Guatemala. After her first birthday, we
6

returned to the States. We've always talked with Raquel about the fact that she's a

Chapina, a Guatemalan—something to be proud _____. We have
7

_____ weavings hanging on the walls. She knows about Rigoberta
8

Menchú, the Nobel Peace Prize _____ from her home country. In
9

order to bring the teaching full _____, we knew this trip was
10

_____.
11

No one is as much a Californian as Raquel. She takes acting classes. She loves

_____. I drive her and her Russian friend Julia to the galleria in
12

Sherman Oaks, drop them _____, and watch as two decked-
13

_____ teenage girls strut to a coffee shop. Raquel tosses her bag
14

higher on her shoulder, slides on sunglasses, and struts away—confident,

_____ to buy new boots. This is her world.
15

"Why do so many kids _____ 16 in Guatemala?" She asked that question years ago. Michelle _____ 17 it, explaining the poverty, the inequalities between rich and _____ 18. "Two of my brothers died, didn't they?" said Raquel. "Yes", said Michelle. "That's why your mother gave you _____ 19, so you would live."

In Poptun, we met up with Chamba, a friend from the '90s. Chamba drove, _____ 20 goats and horses and rusted-out Nissan pickup trucks. "There's your old house," he said. No longer a house, the owner had turned it _____ 21 a mini warehouse to store _____ 22 equipment. We walked in, and it was there that Raquel dropped her camera to her side and wept. It was a _____ 23 that I had never seen before, one that meant to wash into a _____ 24 hole, fill it like a lake.

Two weeks later, we returned home. Raquel took _____ 25 her bed like a fish that's been _____ 26 too many minutes on the side of a pond. She slept for several days. The exhaustion of gap filling—she's adopted, and she's of two cultures, trying to _____ 27 _____ 28 who you are in a world that says you're either this or that. No, girl. You're a little Chapina, and you're the kid who dons the boots and _____ 29 into the mall. Guatemala is your home. California is your home. You don't have to choose one _____ 30 the other. All of it is yours.

A. READING FOR THE MAIN IDEA

Read the editorial. Check the statement that best summarizes the author's main idea.

❑ 1. Rescuing a human being is a laudable act.

❑ 2. African-American children are adopted into Canada because the United States cannot provide a home for them.

❑ 3. The "global child" is not the solution to providing homes to children who need them.

Can Buy Me Love? Why the Private Choice of Adoption Has International Consequences
by Ivy George

As an Indian-American, the adoption of my daughter from India has been a defining experience in our family's life. It has brought deep joys and hopes—and a simultaneous sense of sorrow, not only on her behalf, but for our underlying **complicity** in a world that makes adoptions necessary.

Long before we adopted, I sensed that adopting a child was one of the most **ennobling** acts humans undertake in their personal and public lives. Nothing seems more important than giving life a chance. However, in my exposure to international adoptions in the U.S., I realized that this presumably sacred and primal tie between adult and child was subject to the same corruptions to which other social relations are vulnerable.

The international availability of children lays bare[1] the axes of power in the forms of choice, entitlement, class, and racial privileges located in the global North and West—and those of the powerlessness stemming from massive economic disadvantage, inhospitable cultural and political environments for women, and the effects of human rights abuses from foreign and civil wars in the global South and East.

It is against this backdrop that international adoption takes place. The number of international adoptions in the U.S. rose from 7,093 in 1990 to 22,728 in 2005. More children are adopted into the United States than into any other nation. This dynamic reinforces patterns of dependence and **obscures** more complex global relations. The "Third World" stands as a ready reference to mean poverty, squalor, human abuse, and hopelessness. The child is seen as the one in need and the parents are the rescuers. "Saving" a child out of this **milieu** becomes automatically understood as a sacrificial act. The First World becomes a one-way destination point for children from the global South. There is little effort to understand or affect the local conditions that move people to **relinquish** their children.

I have been struck by the utmost sincerity and **earnestness** of parents of international adoptees, but too often they personalize and privatize their choice. They set out to study Spanish or cook Korean food, even as they work hard to mainstream their children. Indeed, "rescuing" a human being is a **laudable** act, but we must be clear-eyed about the context in which we engage in such action. In the global **nexus** of power relations, Third World societies stand by as a cafeteria—with its produce and people—for satisfying First World needs. It is time to ask hard questions: What is the connection between the availability of children for our adoption and our trade policies that drive their parents into poverty? How do arms sales to the Third World or drug-pricing policies create populations of orphans?

It is difficult to acknowledge that these children provide for some of our deepest human needs at great cost to themselves. The bodies of both the adopted

---

[1]*lays bare:* reveals

(continued)

child and the parents bear the text of devastating **disparities** between two worlds. The parents, by sheer membership in Western society, **manifest** racial, cultural, and national privileges. International adoption assures complete **severance** from the child's native family. The avoidance of any claims from birth parents allows for the total displacement of the child, giving her a "global persona."

Adoptive parents often underestimate the racialized nature of their transaction, especially with the adoption of children who don't resemble them. Many adoption agencies advertise the prospects of forming a "multicultural family"—placing the cultural value of the parents over the effect on the child. Grand visions of multicultural families are further complicated by the **influx** of Asian and Russian children into the U.S. while African-American children are adopted into Canada and Europe because the U.S. cannot provide a home for them.

Here are some considerations for anyone contemplating adopting a child from abroad: International adoption may **exploit** family poverty and gender oppression in the global South and East. The interruption of a child's identification with her racial, ethnic, or national group will have consequences. Many children are made available through abduction, sale, or trafficking. Prevailing trends in international adoption and the construction of the "global child" besmirches[2] an ancient and beautiful response of human beings to protect and provide for the smallest among us. ∎

Reprinted with permission from *Sojourners Magazine*, June 2006. (800) 714-7474.

---

[2]*besmirches*: attacks the good name of

B. READING FOR DETAILS

In her editorial, Ivy George uses both facts and opinions to support her main idea. Read the statements. Next to each statement write *F* if it is a fact or *O* if it is an opinion. Discuss your answers with another student.

_____ 1. Nothing seems more important than giving life a chance.

_____ 2. More children are adopted into the United States than into any other nation.

_____ 3. This dynamic reinforces patterns of dependence and obscures more complex global relations.

_____ 4. There is little effort to understand or affect the local conditions that move people to relinquish their children.

_____ 5. They [parents of international adoptees] set out to study Spanish or cook Korean food, even as they work hard to mainstream their children.

_____ 6. Third World societies stand by as a cafeteria—with its produce and people—for satisfying First World needs.

_____ 7. International adoption assures complete severance from the child's native family.

_____ 8. Many adoption agencies advertise the prospects of forming a "multicultural family"—placing the cultural values of the parents over the effect on the child.

_____ 9. The interruption of a child's identification with her racial, ethnic, or national group will have consequences.

_____10. Many children are made available through abduction, sale, or trafficking.

_____11. Prevailing trends in international adoption and the construction of the "global child" besmirches an ancient and beautiful response of human beings to protect and provide for the smallest among us.

C. WORD SEARCH

Read the following sentences from the editorial. Circle the word or phrase that is closest in meaning to the boldfaced words as they are used in this context.

1. It has brought deep joys and hopes—and a simultaneous sense of sorrow, not on her behalf, but for our underlying **complicity** in a world that makes adoptions necessary.
   a. the act of being involved in a crime with other people
   b. the act of complementing other people
   c. the act of making things more complex

2. Long before we adopted, I sensed that adopting a child was one of the most **ennobling** acts humans undertake in their personal and public lives.
   a. improving one's character
   b. harming one's character
   c. confusing one's character

3. This dynamic reinforces patterns of dependence and **obscures** more complex global relations.
   a. complicates
   b. makes hard to understand
   c. highlights

4. "Saving" a child out of this **milieu** becomes automatically understood as a sacrificial act.
   a. family
   b. setting
   c. country

5. There is little effort to understand or affect the local conditions that move people to **relinquish** their children.
   a. punish
   b. love
   c. give up

6. I have been struck by the utmost sincerity and **earnestness** of parents of international adoptees, but too often they personalize and privatize their choice.
   a. seriousness
   b. desire
   c. deception

7. Indeed, "rescuing" a human being is a **laudable** act, but we must be clear-eyed about the context in which we engage in such action.
   a. heroic
   b. praiseworthy
   c. difficult

8. In the global **nexus** of power relations, Third World societies stand by as a cafeteria—with its produce and people—for satisfying First World needs.
   a. next phase
   b. connection
   c. negativity

9. The bodies of both the adopted child and the parents bear the text of devastating **disparities** between two worlds.
   a. similarities
   b. disadvantages
   c. differences

10. The parents, by sheer membership in Western society, **manifest** racial, cultural, and national privileges. International adoption assures complete severance from the child's native family.
    a. deny
    b. show clearly
    c. reject

11. The parents, by sheer membership in Western society, manifest racial, cultural, and national privileges. International adoption assures complete **severance** from the child's native family.
    a. break
    b. disappearance
    c. understanding

12. Grand visions of "multicultural" families are further complicated by the **influx** of Asian and Russian children into the U.S. while African-American children are adopted into Canada and Europe because the U.S. cannot provide a home for them.
    a. decrease
    b. increase
    c. influence

13. International adoption may **exploit** family poverty and gender oppression in the global South and East.
    a. take advantage of
    b. export
    c. extinguish

A. DISTINGUISHING OPINIONS

Below are six statements by Marcos McPeek Villatoro (1–6) and six by Ivy George (a–f). George's statements reflect a contrasting view, further reflection, or negative side of the views expressed by Villatoro. Match each of George's statements with one by Villatoro. Discuss your choices with a partner.

Villatoro

_____ 1. We've always talked with Raquel about the fact that she's a Chapina, a Guatemalan—something to be proud of.

_____ 2. We have indigenous weavings hanging on the walls. She knows about Rigoberta Menchú, the Nobel Prize winner from her home country.

_____ 3. "Why do so many kids die in Guatemala?" She asked that question years ago. Michelle fielded it, explaining the poverty, the inequalities between rich and poor.

_____ 4. That's why your mother gave you up, so you would live.

_____ 5. The exhaustion of gap filling—she's adopted, and she's of two cultures, trying to figure out who you are in a world that says you're either this or that. . . . Guatemala is your home. California is your home. You don't have to choose one over the other. All of it is yours.

_____ 6. No, girl. You're a little Chapina, and you are the kind of kid who dons the boots and struts into the mall.

George

    a. The child is seen as the one in need and the parents are the rescuers. "Saving" a child out of this milieu becomes automatically understood as a sacrificial act.

    b. It is difficult to acknowledge that these children provide for some of our deepest human needs at great cost to themselves. The bodies of both the adopted child and the parents bear the text of devastating disparities between two worlds. The parents, by sheer membership in Western society, manifest racial, cultural, and national privileges.

    c. Adoptive parents often underestimate the racialized nature of their transaction, especially with the adoption of children who don't resemble them. Many adoption agencies advertise the prospects of forming a "multicultural family"—placing the cultural value of the parents over the effect on the child.

d. International adoption assures complete severance from the child's native family. The avoidance of any claims from birth parents allows for the total displacement of the child, giving her a "global persona."

e. I have been struck by the utmost sincerity and earnestness of parents of international adoptees, but too often they personalize and privatize their choice. They set out to study Spanish or cook Korean food, even as they work hard to mainstream their children.

f. It is time to ask the hard questions: What is the connection between the availability of children for our adoption and our trade policies that drive their parents into poverty? How do arms sales to the Third World or drug-pricing policies create populations of orphans? . . . International adoption may exploit family poverty and gender oppression in the global South and East.

B. GIVING YOUR OPINION

Work in groups. Consider the following themes related to international adoption represented by the statements in Part A. Discuss your opinions of what Villatoro and George say about each.

1. Pride and identity of one's roots

2. Educating international adoptees about the culture of their home country

3. The inequalities between adopting countries and the countries that relinquish their children

4. Saving children from poverty

5. The possibilities of being bicultural

6. Racial identity of adopted children

C. VOCABULARY REINFORCEMENT: Related Words

Work in pairs. Write the number of the word in the first column next to the word in the second column that has a related meaning. Then use the related words to write one or two sentences that summarize something you have learned in the unit. Write a brief explanation of how the matched words are related. The first one has been done for you.

1. manifest   _____ give up

2. disparities   _____ obscure

3. relinquish   _1_ figure out

4. ennobling   _____ gaping hole

5. dodge   _____ earnestness

6. encounter   _____ exploit

7. complicity   _____ nexus

1. In many cases, the differences between a child's birth culture and its adoptive culture are **manifest**. In others, however, it may take the child a while to **figure out** the difference.

    Word relation: Both words are concerned with grasping the truth. If something is **manifest**, it is clearly and obviously true. If you **figure** something **out**, you grasp the truth, but only after an effort.

2. _____

    _____

    Word relation: _____

3. _____

    _____

    Word relation: _____

4. _____

    _____

    Word relation: _____

5. _____

    _____

    Word relation: _____

6. _____

    _____

    Word relation: _____

7. _____

    _____

    Word relation: _____

A. CASE STUDY: Russian Adoptions

The following reading presents recent cases regarding Russian adoptions. It raises the issue of whether international adoptions should be encouraged or even continued. Work in groups. Study the case. Discuss the implications of Russia reopening its overseas adoptions. What policy should Russia set? Present your conclusions to the rest of the class.

Although Russia would prefer to keep its orphans at home, Russian families rarely adopt these children. The country opened adoptions to foreigners in 1990 because there were hundreds of thousands of children waiting to be placed in families. Every year foreigners adopt nearly 8,000 Russian orphans, of which Americans adopt the majority (about 57 percent). Americans adopt more children from Russia than from any other country, except China. There are many reasons why Americans adopt Russian children, but one is that there are very few white American orphans available in the United States, and white families generally prefer to adopt white children.

Lately, however, the adoption situation between Russia and the United States has not been ideal. Since 1990, 12 Russian children have been murdered by their adoptive parents within the United States. These cases caused a backlash in Russia against foreign adoptions. Because Russians cannot control the penalties in the United States when Americans commit crimes against their children, and because their government has had difficulty controlling its adoption process, Russian legislators called for a ban on adoption by foreigners and refused to renew the accreditation of many adoption agencies. As a result, no U.S. adoption agencies are currently accredited in Russia.

Many people are upset by the halting of Russian adoptions and feel that the Russian authorities overreacted. They point out the fact that what happened in these families could have happened to any family, whether the children were adopted or biological. Child abuse happens everywhere and is the exception rather than the rule. The abuse was not because the children had been adopted from Russia, they say. Advocates who support continuing the Russian adoption program say that a child will have a much better chance at a happy, healthy childhood being placed in a foreign family than it will in Russian orphanages, which are often underfunded, overcrowded places where children do not get the attention they need. Children's rights activists have warned that thousands of children will suffer because of this decision. Others are worried about the xenophobia[3] that comes out of this case: the fear of "*our* children from *our* orphanages being adopted by *them*."

Many agree with a temporary halt on Russian adoptions and are calling for reform. Anti-adoption advocates are insisting that the government keep track of all Russian adoptees and be allowed to take action if a Russian orphan becomes a victim of violence after being placed overseas. Yet, these demands appear to be unrealistic. Meanwhile, the government is reconsidering its adoption policy. Should international adoptions be reopened? The Russians would like to get more Russian orphans placed with families in their native country, but this could be a very slow change. The policy needs to be decided in the best interests of the children in Russian orphanages. If these children remain in the orphanages, many of them will not get the education, health care, and loving families that they need.

---

[3]*xenophobia*: extreme fear or hatred of people from other countries

B. DISCUSSION QUESTIONS

Work in groups. Discuss your answers to the questions.

1. Do you agree with Villatoro, that a child does not have to choose one country over another? Is it possible that "all of it" can belong to the adopted child? Or do you agree with George that "forming a 'multi-cultural family' [is] placing the cultural value of the parents over the effect on the child"?

2. Do you think a child adopted from another country should learn about the culture of his or her home country or even return to that country to discover his or her roots? Does this help the child develop a multicultural identity?

VII. WRITING

A. GRAMMAR: Agreement

Notice   Read the following sentences from Ivy George's editorial. Draw a circle around the subject. Draw an arrow to connect the subject to the verb it agrees with. The first one has been done for you.

1. (Nothing) seems more important than giving life a chance.

2. The avoidance of any claims from birth parents allows for the total displacement of the child, giving her a "global persona."

3. There is little effort to understand or affect the local conditions that move people to relinquish their children.

4. Prevailing trends in international adoption and the construction of the "global child" besmirches an ancient and beautiful response of human beings to protect and provide for the smallest among us.

Explanation   In every sentence, the subject must agree with the verb. A singular subject takes a singular verb, and a plural subject takes a plural verb. It is not always obvious to students where this agreement takes place in the sentence.

Cases that sometimes cause confusion:

A. **When the subject is separated from its verb:** When word groups come between the subject and the verb, it can sometimes cause confusion. These word groups may contain a noun that appears to be the subject but in fact modifies the subject. These phrases or clauses have no effect on the subject and verb. Be careful to make the verb agree with its actual subject and not another noun that may be closer to it.

(continued)

In George's sentence 2 above, the verb, *allows*, is singular because the subject, *avoidance*, is singular. (Students often get confused with this type of sentence and may think, for example, that the plural noun, *parents*, is the subject of the verb.)

B. **When indefinite pronouns are used as subjects:** Most indefinite pronouns are treated as singular subjects, even though they may have plural meanings. In formal written English, the following indefinite pronouns are always treated as singular:

anybody	either	neither	nothing
anyone	everybody	no one	somebody
anything	everyone	nobody	someone
each	everything	none	something

In George's sentence 1, the indefinite pronoun subject, *Nothing*, is singular, so the verb, *seems*, is also singular. Marcos McPeek Villatoro's commentary illustrates another example of this type: "**No one is** as much a Californian as Raquel."

C. **When parts of the subject form a single unit:** Usually compound subjects that are joined with *and* are treated as plural subjects:

  Canada and Europe are adopting African-American children from the United States.

However, when two subjects are combined to form a single concept or subject, they are sometimes treated as a singular entity:

  ***Adoptive parents and their children is** the theme of tonight's television series on adoption.*

In the editorial, George combines two ideas to refer to one singular issue as a subject in sentence 4.

D. **When the subject follows the verb:** Verbs typically follow subjects. When the subject follows the verb, it can cause confusion. In sentences beginning with *There is* or *There are*, the subject comes after the verb.

  *There **are** surprisingly many international **adoptees** living in the United States today.*

In sentence 3 of the editorial, the single verb, *is*, is followed by its subject, *effort*.

There are other cases of agreement not illustrated in the editorial that may cause confusion:

E. **When subjects are joined with *or, nor, either . . . or,* or *neither . . . nor*:** Subjects can be connected by *or, nor, either . . . or,* and *neither . . . nor*. There is a special case for these subjects. The verb agrees with the noun closest to the verb. For example:

  *A single parent or **two parents** under the age of 50 **are** able to adopt a child in China.*
  *Either Russia or **China has** recently been the country to send the most orphans to the United States.*
  *Neither Rachel nor her **parents feel** that she should have to choose a country to call "home."*

F. **When nouns "look" plural but are actually singular in meaning:** Some nouns are singular, despite their plural form. These words often refer to collective bodies or academic disciplines:

  *The **United States adopts** more children than any other country.*
  *The **news** about international adoption **is** alarming.*
  *Statistics **is** my favorite course!*

(Notice how when this subject refers to separate items, it is used as a plural noun: "**Statistics show** that international adoptions are falling.")

G. **When collective nouns are singular unless the meaning is clearly plural:** Some nouns are singular in naming a group: *class, committee, couple, government*. They emphasize the group as a unit. If the individual members of a collective noun are emphasized, it may be plural:

*The **committee are** currently debating possible changes to adoption laws[4].*

The phrase *the number* is treated as singular; *a number* is treated as plural:

*The **number** of overseas adoptions **is** declining.*
*A **number** of overseas adoptions **are** being called into question.*

---

[4]This usage is more common in British English.

Exercise 1

Circle the correct form of the verb in each sentence.

1. The news (has / have) recently reported that international adoptions are dropping off.

2. None of the recent international adoptees (has / have) been Korean, as Korea has put a limit on overseas adoptions.

3. It is hard to know whether international adoption is successful. The pros and cons (is / are) still being debated.

4. A number of children adopted by Americans (comes / come) from overseas countries such as Guatemala, Russia, and China.

5. Either the Internet or the newspapers (reports / report) recent statistics concerning international adoptions.

6. There (is / are) many sociologists who think that international adoptions cause an interruption of a child's racial and cultural identity.

7. Economics (is / are) the best field of study to understand the effect of the First World on the Third World.

8. There are fewer babies available for international adoption to the United States. One of the reasons (is / are) the cooperating nations' recent ability to better care for their children.

9. Both China and Russia (has / have) recently made international adoptions to the United States more difficult.

10. Everybody (considers / consider) what life might be without children at some point in their life.

Exercise 2

Each sentence contains an error in subject–verb agreement. Find and correct the errors.

1. The news in all of today's papers say that a new international agreement will forbid American couples from adopting in certain areas of the world.

2. Everyone hearing this news and wanting to adopt children from abroad realize that their chances to adopt will be limited.

3. Neither the adopted child nor the adoptive parents has an easy time dealing with adolescence, when all children question their identity.

4. One of the most important aspects were whether the parents would be comfortable raising children that did not resemble them.

5. The child's pride and self-esteem has been restored since he was adopted into that family.

6. There has been many adopted children around the world that have never learned about their family or cultural origins.

7. None of the parents over the age of 50 are allowed to adopt a baby in China.

8. The "new family," the one composed of internationally adopted children, are perhaps representative of the future.

9. Those kinds of adoptions is very sad.

10. In developing countries, the poor does not always have enough money to support their children and often give them up.

B. WRITING STYLE: Introductions and Conclusions

Notice Notice the way George, the author of "Can Buy Me Love? Why the Private Choice of Adoption Has International Consequences," introduces and concludes her editorial.

a. What does George do to introduce her editorial?

b. How is her conclusion the same as or different from her introduction?

Explanation An effective introduction will catch the reader's attention and give him or her an idea of the direction the essay will take through the thesis statement.

George captures her reader's attention by sharing some facts about her own family's experience. She uses a brief anecdote to draw readers into the issues of international adoption. She then states her thesis: her "sorrow, not only on her behalf, but for our underlying complicity in a world that makes adoptions necessary." We know from this statement that she will explore the negative side of international adoption.

George concludes her essay by returning to the idea she expressed in her introduction. But she does more than just repeat what she said in the introduction. She repeats the idea that international adoptions have their downside but then gives advice to those who may be considering adopting a child from abroad.

An effective conclusion will often repeat the writer's thesis in a different way and take a new view of the same idea in order to leave the reader thinking.

There are many different ways to introduce an essay:

A. **Facts and statistics:** Introducing an essay with some surprising facts or interesting statistics can capture the reader's attention.

B. **Short generalization:** A simple sentence that catches the reader's attention and introduces the topic can sometimes be the most effective introduction.

C. **Historical reference:** A useful way to introduce a topic is to provide some historical information about it. Historical reference can often provide relevant background information to show the importance of the topic being discussed.

D. **Example or anecdote:** An example or short description of an event or story can be an effective introduction to an essay when it illustrates the thesis that will be developed by the writer.

E. **Questions:** Questions can also pique the reader's interest. By posing one or more questions in the introduction, the writer can involve the reader and set up a structure for the development of the essay.

F. **Quotation:** Sometimes the words of others can best introduce a topic. If a quotation introduces a thesis in a unique way, this could be an effective beginning.

There are also many ways to conclude an essay:

G. **Summary:** One of the most typical (though not always the most interesting) ways to conclude an essay is to summarize the main points that have been discussed in the essay. (If this type of conclusion is used, try to avoid simplistic expressions such as *in conclusion, in summary,* and *finally.*)

H. **Example / anecdote:** Ending with an example or story that illustrates the thesis can be a powerful way to conclude an essay.

I. **Quotations:** A quotation can sometimes best sum up a writer's thesis. Someone else's words are sometimes the strongest way to conclude an essay.

(continued)

J. **Call for action:** Giving advice or ending with a plea for action is sometimes the most appropriate ending. With this type of conclusion, readers are left thinking about their responsibility for acting on what has been discussed in the essay.

K. **Questions:** Leaving readers with questions that remain to be answered can be a strong ending. If an essay has explored a problem but has not offered a particular solution, this might be an effective conclusion.

L. **Prediction or own conclusion:** Writers may choose to conclude their essays by making a prediction about the future; or, after analyzing a problem, the writer may draw his or her own conclusion about it.

Exercise

Read the paragraphs. Determine whether they are introductions or conclusions. Which technique described on pages 61–62 is used in each one? Write the letter (A–L) that corresponds to the technique.

_____ 1. After examining the experiences of these multicultural families, we have seen that international adoption is one of the best ways to combat racism. As Elizabeth Bartholet from Harvard University said, "There's very little evidence to the racial and national essentialist[5] claim. If we discourage international adoption, we encourage surrogacy[6], we encourage medical interventions. We're encouraging white people to reproduce white people. It's racial bias."

_____ 2. At the age of 41, Samantha realized that she did not need a husband to experience motherhood. Even though she had not yet found a suitable marriage partner, she could not envision her life without children. On September 20, Samantha boarded a plane to Beijing, where she would spend two months waiting to adopt her baby. In November, she was back home starting her life as a single mom. Like Samantha, more and more women are deciding to create a family on their own.

_____ 3. For the first time in over a decade, the number of international adoptions in the United States has decreased. From 2005 to 2006, there were 2,049 fewer adoptions by Americans. Korean adoptions decreased by 15 percent; adoptions from mainland China dropped by 18 percent that same year; Ukraine adoptions were cut almost in half, from 821 to 460. Many countries are expressing new concerns over the welfare of adopted children as well as the trafficking of babies, which accounts for the reduction in international adoptions.

---

[5]*essentialist*: belief that members of races or nationalities all have certain definite characteristics
[6]*surrogacy*: act of serving as a substitute parent

_____ 4. Adopting children from overseas can create the ideal multicultural family. Yet, as we have seen, it is not without issues. Before parents adopt a child from another country, they must consider the child's identity. How will he or she feel about his or her race? What relationship, if any, will the child have to his or her home country? Will the child want to meet his or her birth parents? How will you respond?

_____ 5. Based on the concerns discussed above, the Hague Convention could cause fewer children to be placed in loving families: Many countries have not yet ratified the treaty. There are not enough qualified attorneys to handle the applications for inter-country adoptions. Certain governments are ill-equipped to collect the required data on the children being put up for adoption. Although the Convention's goal is to make international adoptions safer, more children will suffer as a result of these problems.

_____ 6. The goal of international adoption is to find a home for each orphaned child, not to "produce" a child for a family. This objective must be considered before parents go overseas to adopt a baby.

_____ 7. The adoption of children from other countries to the United States began in the 1940s, when Japanese and European children were orphaned during World War II. War was also the reason children were adopted by American families from Greece in the late 1940s, from Korea in the 1950s, and from Vietnam in the 1960s and 1970s. Today, poverty, more than war, explains the number of overseas adoptions.

C. ESSAY QUESTIONS

Write an essay on one of the topics. Use ideas, vocabulary, and writing techniques from this unit.

1. "National boundaries should not prevent abandoned children from having families."
   (Thomas Atwood, President of America's National Council for Adoption)

   To what extent do you agree or disagree with this quote? Write an essay in which you express your opinion.

2. Why are international adoptions on the decrease today? Why are many countries deciding to limit the number of children they send out for overseas adoptions? Is this new trend good or bad, in your opinion? Write an essay in which you explain your opinion.

Beyond Darwin

AS YOU CAN SEE FROM YOUR GENETIC PRINTOUT YOU ONLY THINK YOU'RE DEPRESSED WHEREAS YOU ARE IN FACT A JOLLY, HAPPY FULL OF THE JOYS OF SPRING TYPE PERSON!

http://www.cartoonstock.com

I. ANTICIPATING THE ISSUE

Discuss your answers to the questions.

1. Look at the title. Look at the cartoon. What do you think the issue of this unit will be?

2. What is the message or humor of the cartoon?

3. How do you feel about experimentation with human genes?

Read the text.

Recent advances in technology have allowed researchers to make great progress in genetic engineering. As we learn more about our genetic makeup and ways to **manipulate** genes to treat disease, we also raise ethical issues and create challenges related to privacy and discrimination. Who will have access to our genetic information, and what will be done with it once they have it? The **ramifications** of access to such information and its uses are enormous.

Current research into the human gene system is helping us understand why people have **predispositions** to certain diseases. Knowing our genetic makeup can help us **gauge** whether we may be **stricken** by a particular illness, such as cancer. Even before birth, we are able to do genetic **screenings** to determine what a child's genetic disorders will be. The Human Genome Project, a $3 trillion government-sponsored program, cataloged the genomes of tens of thousands of humans and other species. Scientists have already isolated and identified the genes responsible for the more than 4,000 genetic diseases that affect human beings.

The implications of this knowledge are **staggering**. In addition to predicting genetic predispositions toward diseases, gene therapies may provide new treatments or cures for serious diseases. Millions of people already use genetically engineered drugs to treat heart disease, cancer, AIDS, and strokes. With the research that is now being conducted, we may find cures to many more diseases.

In the near future, genetic experimentation will also allow parents to select the traits of their children. Genetic traits that determine height, weight, and eye and hair color will be able to be controlled, and many parents are excited about this potential.

Many people, however, are **reluctant** to embrace the possibilities that genetic research allows. They fear the **specter** of genetic discrimination. For example, one reason some women do not use the latest genetic testing for breast cancer is because they are afraid of discrimination by insurance companies. Another problem is that many people do not want to discover their weaknesses. What if they learn that they have a disease for which there are no medical **interventions**? How will such knowledge affect their lives? Do people really want to know how they might die?

Many believe we have not always shown **stellar** decision making in our ethical choices. Jeremy Rifkin is probably the best known opponent of genetic engineering. He believes that we are not responsible enough to experiment with genes and should not "play God." He asks, "Just because it can be done, does that mean it should be done?" He claims that everyone will eventually look and act the same if parents select the traits of their children, and he questions the desirability of such a society.

One fear about genetic experimentation involves privacy. Already, blood samples taken in hospitals have been used for research without patients' consent. Most people would agree that one's health and genetic makeup are private concerns. But if insurance companies gain access to this information, it could have a large impact on insurance coverage or costs; if employers can obtain the data, it could affect hiring or promotion decisions. The possibilities for discrimination are obvious.

Genetic research will continue to reveal secrets about the human body, but at what cost? Will these discoveries indeed lead to progress in improving the human condition?

A. VOCABULARY

Match the boldfaced words and phrases in the Background Reading with their definitions or synonyms below. Write the word or phrase next to its definition.

1. _____: change; move; develop

2. _____: estimate; judge

3. _____: unwilling; resistant

4. _____: brilliant

5. _____: astonishing; overwhelming

6. _____: consequences

7. _____: haunting fear of future trouble

8. _____: tests to detect unwanted attribute

9. _____: interference to stop something

10. _____: states of mind or body favorable to (something)

11. _____: afflicted; attacked

B. SUMMARIZING THE ISSUE

Work in small groups. Summarize the issue presented in the Background Reading. Write positive outcomes of genetic experimentation in the left circle, negative examples in the right circle, and outcomes that could be both positive and negative in the middle.

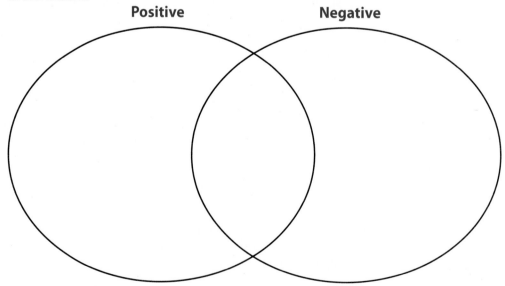

Positive   Negative

C. VALUES CLARIFICATION

Work in small groups. Discuss your answers to the questions.

1. Do you see genetic experimentation as valuable?

2. Should there be a limit to genetic experimentation? If so, at what point?

III. OPINION 1: LISTENING

A. LISTENING FOR THE MAIN IDEAS

Listen to the commentary and circle the best answer to each question.

1. What does commentator Lauren Weinstein mention as a positive outcome of genetic technology?
   a. the ability to choose traits for our children
   b. the ability to create new treatments for serious diseases
   c. the ability to predict possible health problems for children

2. What is Weinstein's biggest concern about future genetic technology?
   a. There won't be enough genetic screenings for everyone to benefit.
   b. People who should get tested will not get tested.
   c. We don't know who will have access to our genetic information.

B. LISTENING FOR DETAILS

Listen again. According to the commentary, does the information reflect something science can already do or something it will be able to do in the future? Check *Now* or *Future*. Compare your answers with those of another student. Listen again if necessary.

	NOW	FUTURE
A gene can predict the life span of a human.		
Predispositions to disease can be gauged.		
We can create custom-made babies.		
Medical screening procedures can predict which disease one might suffer from.		
Gene therapies offer new treatments for various diseases.		
There is genetic discrimination by insurance companies and employers.		
We can limit who knows our genetic makeup.		

Read the commentary. Fill in the missing words. Then listen again to check your answers. If your answers differ from the commentary, ask your teacher if they are acceptable alternatives.

Introduction

When scientists in Hawaii _____ out how to clone mice earlier this
                              1
week, some researchers said that the technology to clone humans may only be five

years away. Commentator Lauren Weinstein believes that these kinds of scientific

advances _____ more questions than answers.
              2

Commentary

In the classic science fiction story "Lifeline," author Robert A. Heinlein described a

machine which could _____ the date of a person's death. The
                           3
impact of such _____ were complicated in the story and may well turn
                      4
out to be even more complex in real life. It's been announced that a gene has been

found which may predict the maximum _____ for an individual.
                                              5

Unlike the machine in Heinlein's story, genes of course won't tell us if we're

going to be hit by a truck, and genetic _____ can't take into account
                                               6
lifestyle influences—diet, smoking, and so on—which can impact our health and

life span. But the approximately 80,000 genes of our DNA, making up the very

_____ of our beings, can be used to _____
        7   **8**
predispositions to disease and other life factors.

The Human Genome Project, an international effort, has _____
                                                              9
out more than 6,000 human genes with a goal of mapping and understanding

them all. The _____ are staggering. It may be possible in the future
                     10
to _____ genetic structures to create custom-made babies with any
        11
desired set of traits: high intelligence, physical strength, zebra _____?
                                                                          12
The _____ of such power raise ethical and moral dilemmas of
          13

great import. Shivers down the _____ might be in order. Mankind's
                                      14

judgment when it comes to dealing with powerful technologies has not always been

_____, to say the least.
        15

In the short run, there are other genetic possibilities and concerns. Genetic

knowledge is creating medical screening procedures which can be used to predict

whether or not you're likely to _____ with certain kinds of cancers or
                                        16

other diseases. These tests don't usually provide 100 percent _____,
                                                                        17

but many are extremely accurate.

Knowledge of disease _____ can lead to more frequent examinations
                              18

or tests and life-saving early interventions. Gene therapies _____ the
                                                                      19

promise of exciting new treatments for various serious diseases. But sometimes what

to do with such knowledge isn't clear _____.
                                              20

It's not easy to deal with _____ predictions of contracting a
                                  21

disease for which there's no effective treatment or estimates regarding possible

health problems in future children. Since such genetic information generally is

presented as a set of _____ odds, not absolute certainties, some very
                              22

difficult situations can result.

For many persons, this may drive a _____ to undergo genetic
                                            23

_____ at all. Even many in the genetic and medical fields are worried
        24

that inappropriate use of genetic screening tests, perhaps as part of

_____ blood workups, could do more harm than good. There are
        25

questions regarding the accuracy and interpretation of results from some genetic

tests and the possibly needless _____ of patients.
                                        26

Then there's the _____ of genetic discrimination, concerns over
                        27

insurance companies, employers, and others who could _____ against
                                                              28

people who *have* diseases—bad enough—but also against those whose genetic tests

suggest they *might* be likely to _____ diseases in the future.
₂₉

As individuals and as a society, we need to take active stands about how our

genetic information is collected, studied, _____, and used. We've
₃₀

created a crystal ball into our genetic _____. We'd better start
₃₁

deciding right now who is going to be peering inside.

IV. OPINION 2: READING

A. READING FOR THE MAIN IDEAS

Read the editorial. Check the arguments that Watson uses to present his main idea.

- ❑ 1. Human biology is now as powerful as physics.
- ❑ 2. Research might best be ruled by strong regulations.
- ❑ 3. Recombinant-DNA is probably the safest technology ever developed.
- ❑ 4. We should postpone dangerous experiments with genes.
- ❑ 5. We are falling behind if we don't start to manipulate DNA.
- ❑ 6. We must be careful of scientists trying to create "superpersons."
- ❑ 7. Gene-bettered children are desirable, not a threat.
- ❑ 8. Human evolution is unfair.

All for the Good
Why Genetic Engineering Must Soldier On
by James D. Watson[1] . . . .

There is lots of zip in DNA-based biology today. With each passing year it incorporates an ever increasing fraction of the life sciences, ranging from single-cell organisms, like bacteria and yeast, to the complexities of the human brain. All this wonderful biological **frenzy** was unimaginable when I first entered the world of genetics. In 1948, biology was

[1]James Watson and Francis Crick won a Nobel Prize for medicine for their 1953 discovery of the structure of DNA. Watson was the first director of the Human Genome Project; he now serves as president of Cold Spring Harbor Laboratory.

an all too descriptive discipline near the bottom of science's **totem pole**, with physics at its top. By then Einstein's turn-of-the-century ideas about the interconversion of matter and energy had been transformed into the powers of the atom. If not **held in check**, the weapons they made possible might well destroy the very fabric of civilized human life. So physicists of the late 1940s were simultaneously **revered** for making atoms relevant to society and feared for what their toys could do if they were to fall into the hands of evil.

Such **ambivalent** feelings are now widely held toward biology. The double-helical structure of DNA, initially admired for its intellectual simplicity, today represents to many a **double-edged sword** that can be used for evil as well as good. No sooner had scientists at Stanford University in 1973 begun rearranging DNA molecules in test tubes (and, equally important, reinserting the novel DNA segments back into living cells) than critics began likening these "recombinant" DNA procedures to the physicist's power to break apart atoms. Might not some of the test-tube-rearranged DNA molecules impart to their host cells disease-causing capacities that, like nuclear weapons, are capable of seriously disrupting human civilization? Soon there were cries from both scientists and nonscientists that such research might best be ruled by **stringent** regulations—if not laws.

As a result, several years were to pass before the full power of recombinant-DNA technology got into the hands of working scientists, who by then were **itching to** explore previously unattainable secrets of life. Happily, the proposals to control recombinant-DNA scenarios failed to materialize; even the modestly restrictive governmental regulations began to **wither away**. In retrospect, recombinant-DNA may rank as the safest revolutionary technology ever developed. To my knowledge, not one **fatality**, much less illness, has been caused by a genetically manipulated organism.

The moral I draw from this painful episode is this: Never postpone experiments that have clearly defined future benefits for fear of dangers that can't be quantified. Though it may sound at first uncaring, we can react rationally only to real (as opposed to hypothetical) risks. Yet for several years we postponed important experiments on the genetic basis of cancer, for example, because we took much too seriously **spurious** arguments that the genes at the root of human cancer might themselves be dangerous to work with.

Though most forms of DNA manipulation are now effectively unregulated, one important potential goal remains blocked. Experiments aimed at learning how to insert functional genetic material into human germ cells—sperm and eggs—remain off-limits to most of the world's scientists. No governmental body wants to take responsibility for initiating steps that might help redirect the course of future human evolution.

These decisions reflect widespread concerns that we, as humans, may not have the wisdom to modify the most precious of all human treasures—our chromosomal "instruction books." Dare we be entrusted with improving upon the results of the several million years of Darwinian natural selection? Are human germ cells Rubicons that geneticists may never cross[2]?

Unlike many of my peers, I'm reluctant to accept such reasoning, again using the argument that you should never put off doing something useful for fear of evil that may never arrive. The first germ-line gene manipulations are unlikely to be attempted for **frivolous** reasons. Nor does the state of today's science provide the knowledge that would be needed to generate "superpersons" whose far-ranging talents would make those who are genetically unmodified feel redundant and unwanted. Such creations will remain denizens[3] of science fiction, not the real world, far into the future. When they are finally attempted, germ-line genetic manipulations will probably be done to change a death sentence into a life verdict—by creating children who are resistant to a deadly virus, for example, much the way we can already protect plants from viruses by inserting antiviral DNA segments into their genomes.

If appropriate go-ahead signals come, the first resulting gene-bettered children will in no sense threaten human civilization. They will be seen as special only by those in their immediate circles and are likely to pass as unnoticed in later life as the now grown-up "test-tube baby" Louise Brown[4] does today. If they grow up healthily gene-bettered, more such children will follow, and they and those whose lives are enriched by their existence will rejoice that science has again improved human life. If, however, the added genetic material fails to work, better procedures must be developed before more couples commit their **psyches** toward such inherently unsettling pathways to producing healthy children.

Moving forward will not be for the faint of heart. But if the next century witnesses failure, let it be because our science is not yet up to the job, not because we don't have the courage to make less random the sometimes most unfair courses of human evolution. ∎

From *Time*, January 11, 1999. © 1999 Time Inc. Reprinted by permission.

[2]*cross the Rubicon*: do something important that cannot be changed
[3]*denizens*: inhabitans (plants, animal, or human)
[4]*Louise Brown*: first baby to be conceived outside a woman's body

Answer the questions with information from James D. Watson's editorial.

1. Which scientific discipline was most important in 1948?

   _____

2. How were physicists judged in the late 1940s because of their work in atomic energy?

   _____ and _____

3. What scientific parallel did people draw to recombinant-DNA technology?

   _____

4. What dreaded outcome would the rearranging of DNA contribute to, according to critics?

   _____

5. What kinds of restrictions or controls are there over DNA manipulation today?

   _____

6. Which genetic material is still off-limits to genetic research because of its potential danger?

   _____

7. What type of genetic work are governments unwilling to do?

   _____

8. What concept will always remain science fiction, according to Watson?

   _____

9. Where do we already successfully manipulate DNA to prevent disease?

   _____

10. How will gene-bettered children eventually be regarded in later life?

   _____

11. What should be done if manipulated DNA is unsuccessful?

   _____

C. WORD SEARCH

Read the sentences from the editorial. Circle the word or phrase that is closest in meaning to the boldfaced words as they are used in this context.

1. All this wonderful biological **frenzy** was unimaginable when I first entered the world of genetics.
   a. distress
   b. sleepiness
   c. violent excitement

2. In 1948, biology was an all too descriptive discipline near the bottom of science's **totem pole**, with physics at its top.
   a. hierarchy
   b. research capability
   c. symbol

3. If not **held in check**, the weapons they made possible might well destroy the very fabric of civilized human life.
   a. verified
   b. improved
   c. controlled

4. So physicists of the late 1940s were simultaneously **revered** for making atoms relevant to society and feared for what their toys could do if they were to fall into the hands of evil.
   a. criticized
   b. admired
   c. questioned

5. Such **ambivalent** feelings are now widely held toward biology.
   a. negative
   b. positive
   c. uncertain

6. The double-helical structure of DNA, initially admired for its intellectual simplicity, today represents to many a **double-edged sword** that can be used for evil as well as good.
   a. a thing that is both positive and negative
   b. a thing that is twice as harmful
   c. a thing that is positive though seemingly negative

7. Soon there were cries from both scientists and nonscientists that such research might best be ruled by **stringent** regulations—if not laws.
   a. less severe
   b. strict
   c. new

8. As a result, several years were to pass before the full power of recombinant-DNA technology got into the hands of working scientists, who by then were **itching to** explore previously unattainable secrets of life.
   a. eager to
   b. hoping to
   c. planning to

9. Happily, the proposals to control recombinant-DNA scenarios failed to materialize; even the modestly restrictive governmental regulations began to **wither away**.
   a. fade
   b. gain popularity
   c. move

10. To my knowledge, not one **fatality**, much less illness, has been caused by a genetically manipulated organism.
    a. mistake
    b. disease
    c. death

11. Yet for several years we postponed important experiments on the genetic basis of cancer, for example, because we took much too seriously **spurious** arguments that the genes at the root of human cancer might themselves be dangerous to work with.
    a. solid
    b. false
    c. well-researched

12. The first germ-line gene manipulations are unlikely to be attempted for **frivolous** reasons.
    a. personal
    b. experimental
    c. not serious

13. If, however, the added genetic material fails to work, better procedures must be developed before more couples commit their **psyches** toward such inherently unsettling pathways to producing healthy children.
    a. money
    b. minds
    c. energies

A. DISTINGUISHING OPINIONS

Below are five opinions Lauren Weinstein expressed in his commentary (1–5). Match each of Weinstein's opinions with an opposed view from James D. Watson's editorial (a–e). Discuss your choices with a partner.

Weinstein

_____ 1. It may be possible to create custom-made babies with any desired set of traits. . . . Shivers down the spine might be in order.

_____ 2. Mankind's judgment when dealing with powerful technologies has not always been stellar.

_____ 3. To know what to do with the knowledge of disease predispositions isn't clear-cut.

_____ 4. Genetic discrimination will occur once we start improving human genes.

_____ 5. We need to take an active stand about how genetic knowledge will be used.

Watson

a. In retrospect, recombinant-DNA may rank as the safest revolutionary technology ever developed. To my knowledge, not one fatality, much less illness, has been caused by a genetically manipulated organism.

b. Never postpone experiments that have clearly defined future benefits for fear of dangers that can't be quantified. Though it may sound at first uncaring, we can react rationally only to real (as opposed to hypothetical) risks.

c. Unlike many of my peers, I'm reluctant to accept such reasoning, again using the argument that you should never put off doing something useful for fear of evil that may never arrive.

d. Nor does the state of today's science provide the knowledge that would be needed to generate "superpersons" whose far-ranging talents would make those who are genetically unmodified feel redundant and unwanted.

e. If appropriate go-ahead signals come, the first resulting gene-bettered children will in no sense threaten human civilization. They will be seen as special only by those in their immediate circles and are likely to pass as unnoticed in later life as the now grown-up "test-tube baby" Louise Brown does today.

Circle the opinions in Part A that match your own opinions. Discuss your choices with classmates.

C. VOCABULARY REINFORCEMENT: Word Forms

Work in small groups. Fill in the missing word forms for each vocabulary item in the chart. (An *X* has been placed in the box if there is no related word form.) Use a dictionary if necessary.

NOUNS	VERBS	ADJECTIVES
	X	ambivalent
fatality	X	
frenzy	X	
	manipulate	
	X	frivolous
reluctance	X	
		revered
		stricken
	X	stringent

Complete the sentences with the correct word from the chart. There may be more than one correct answer.

1. According to Watson, not one _____ mistake has been made by a genetically manipulated organism.

2. Medical screening procedures may actually be able to predict which

   diseases may _____ us at a given point in our life.

3. _____ DNA protects plants from certain viruses, so why shouldn't we consider doing it for humans?

4. Because many people are _____ about learning the truth, they may never get genetic screenings.

5. The controversy over genetic engineering has developed between fearful citizens who doubt humankind's ability to manage progress and

   _____ scientists who are competing to collect, study, and catalog the human genes.

6. Will gene manipulation become a _____ act, with people changing their genes only for their pleasure?

7. Some genetic scientists feel a certain _____ about their work: They feel the need to seek knowledge that will help cure diseases, but they also fear that their discoveries could be misused or abused in tomorrow's society.

8. Will _____ laws be enough to keep science from progressing?

9. In modern times scientists have usually enjoyed the greatest

   _____ from the public, but now that their work raises ethical issues, they are sometimes criticized.

VI. SPEAKING

A. CASE STUDY: The Ashkenazic[5] Community

The following reading presents a true case that raises the issue of whether human genes should be manipulated.

Work in small groups. Study the case. Put yourselves in the role of the Ashkenazic women who have been asked to participate in the cancer research project. Consider the different perspectives of these women, their history, and the comments made by scientists and doctors. Decide whether or not you will participate in the research. Present your decision to the rest of the class.

Research has shown that Ashkenazic Jewish women may have a predisposition to breast and ovarian cancer. A higher risk of cancer is associated with mutations in the BRCA1 and BRCA2 genes, which have been found in this population of women. Scientists were able to find these cancer-causing alterations in this group because it is easier to locate alterations in ethnic-specific populations that tend to intermarry and that have a complete family history.

   Similar genetic research is being conducted in other populations where people choose to intermarry or where people live in geographically isolated places in the world. The Amish

[5]Ashkenazic Jews are Yiddish-speaking Jews of eastern European origin.

(continued)

and Mormon groups in the United States have been studied because of their tradition of intermarriage. Northern countries such as Finland, Iceland, and Norway have been ideal genetic research areas because of their geographical remoteness. In Finland and Iceland, the gene pools have remained relatively unchanged for 1,000 years; such homogeneity offers researchers the opportunity to trace the genetics of complex diseases. In Iceland, for example, Swiss pharmaceutical companies have collaborated in a twelve-year, $12-million genetic research project that will help develop drugs to combat genetically caused diseases. The Ashkenazic Jews have a similar profile to these geographically isolated populations in that they have tended not to marry outside of their own group.

The Ashkenazic women have been urged to take part in genetic tests that may benefit them as well as people around the world. Much more information is needed to help determine the genetic causes of cancer. But while many Jewish women are interested in participating in this research, many others have been unwilling to donate their blood for research because of privacy issues. These women, fearing that they will be singled out as "genetically flawed," have raised concerns about discrimination in insurance or employment. They point to discrimination cases from the 1970s, when African Americans were denied insurance because they are prone to sickle-cell anemia, a genetic disease. They wonder whether similar cases might not apply to them.

In addition to fears of discrimination, some Ashkenazic women have questioned whether there will be any personal medical benefit to knowing that they have a mutation for a cancer-causing gene. Although some doctors believe that knowing about a mutation through early screening could improve one's prognosis, others feel that there is no proof that mutations could be changed to reduce or prevent disease. Many of the Ashkenazic women simply do not want to know about their genetic makeup if there is nothing they can do to improve it.

A meeting was held by Hadassah, the largest Jewish membership organization in the United States, and the Jewish Council for Public Affairs in hopes that the Jewish community would feel less reluctant to participate in the research. A dialogue between Jewish community leaders and prominent scientists was initiated. At the meeting, scientists maintained that there is no evidence that the Ashkenazic population has a higher probability of getting cancer than any other population. According to Dr. Francis Collins, head of the National Human Genome Research Institute, "we are all walking around with flaws." Collins claimed that there was no evidence that "genetic flaws are greater for one population than another," and he said "there are no perfect specimens."

The discussions and debates continue. The Ashkenazic women's ambivalence must be resolved. Either they will agree or disagree to continue their participation in this genetic research.

B. DISCUSSION QUESTIONS

Work in groups. Discuss your answers to the questions.

1. A recent article on genetics made the following statement:

   Thinking genetically makes us say that the problem is not ours as a society but yours as an individual.

   What does this statement mean? To what extent do you agree or disagree with it? Give examples to support your view.

2. In the not-too-distant future, judges and juries may have to struggle with making decisions related to genetic information. For example, genetic tests are already used for identifying criminals as well as victims of tragedies. In the near future, discrimination lawsuits may end up in courts as a result of the misuse of genetic information.

Should genetic information be made public? When considering genetic information, where do you draw the line between personal privacy and the public's right to know?

VII. WRITING

A. GRAMMAR: Count and Noncount Nouns

Notice Notice the highlighted nouns in the following sentence from the commentary. Which are count nouns and which are noncount nouns? Can any of the nouns be both count and noncount?

*The **ramifications** of such **power** raise ethical and moral **dilemmas** of great **import**.*

Explanation *Countable* and *uncountable* refer to different kinds of nouns. Countable nouns are sometimes called *count nouns*. Uncountable nouns are sometimes called *noncount nouns* or *mass nouns*. Some nouns can also be countable in one meaning and / or usage and uncountable in another.

In the example, *ramifications* and *dilemmas* are count nouns.

Both *power* and *import* can be either count or noncount, but the meaning changes in the two forms:

Power as a noncount noun, as it is used above, refers to "the ability to control." In its countable form, *power / powers* can refer to a faculty of the body or mind or "legal right."

Import as a noncount noun refers to importance. But in its countable form, *import / imports* refers to "goods from a foreign country."

Many words, such as *power* and *import*, have both countable and uncountable meanings. Substances, materials, activities, and abstract ideas often have countable meanings when they are given boundaries.

Exercise 1

Work with a partner. Decide whether each noun is count (C), noncount (NC), or can be either count or noncount (C / NC). Label each one accordingly. Use a dictionary if necessary.

_____ 1. body   _____ 8. discrimination

_____ 2. impact   _____ 9. society

_____ 3. wisdom   _____ 10. state

_____ 4. specimen   _____ 11. profile

_____ 5. intelligence   _____ 12. knowledge

_____ 6. reluctance   _____ 13. fatality

_____ 7. harm   _____ 14. genetics

Exercise 2

The following sentences contain nouns that are both count and noncount. Their meanings change according to whether they are in the count or noncount form. Underline the correct form based on the context of each sentence.

1. Commentator Lauren Weinstein seems to be anxious because he has (concern / concerns) about the direction in which we are headed with genetic science.

2. Of all the (science / sciences) in today's modern world, biology seems to present the most ethical issues.

3. In recent years, there has been an increase in deep ethical (matter / matters) being discussed by genetic scientists.

4. Today many people die of terminal diseases, but it is possible that more (life / lives) will be saved with the help of genetic engineering.

5. Are scientists committing (evil / evils) by doing research that could lead to the betterment of humankind?

6. Pharmaceutical drugs produced from genetic engineering could soon become a significant part of the (good / goods) bought and sold in commercial markets.

7. In what (state / states) will future generations be when they have the power to alter lives through genetic research?

8. New treatments may reduce the (fatality / fatalities) of diseases such as cancer.

9. Recent advances in biological science have given filmmakers good (material/materials) for science fiction movies.

B. WRITING STYLE: Paragraph Cohesion

Notice   Notice the way James D. Watson connects his ideas in his editorial. What are some techniques he uses to connect each new paragraph to the preceding one? How does he maintain the flow of his ideas between paragraphs? Can you see any words or phrases that indicate an "old idea," something already mentioned, in the first sentence of a new paragraph?

Explanation   In each topic sentence of the body of his editorial, Watson refers back to an idea he has mentioned in the previous paragraph, an "old idea," before introducing a "new idea."

Not every topic sentence of a paragraph must be tightly tied to the ideas of the preceding paragraph. However, in essay writing, we should look for opportunities to allude to the subject of a previous paragraph in a new topic sentence. The shift from one topic to the next should be smooth, not abrupt.

There are two basic ways to connect paragraphs smoothly in an essay:

Transitions: Transitional phrases can be used to introduce a new idea or new paragraph in the body of an essay. Some transitional phrases are:

As a result . . .
Second, consider the issue of . . .
An additional example is . . .

Repetition: Another way of picking up an old idea while introducing a new idea is to repeat key words and phrases. Repetitions can be done in several ways:

• Use the same words or phrases from the previous paragraph
• Use pronouns to refer back to a subject
• Use the same words or phrases but in a different form
• Paraphrase ideas from the previous paragraph

(continued)

Certain structures and words may be useful in using this technique:

Not only . . . but also . . .
While X is, Y is . . .
Although X, Y . . .
Unlike (Like) X, Y . . .
such
this

Exercise 1

Examine the first sentence of each paragraph in Watson's editorial. Then look at the paragraph that precedes it. What is the old idea? What is the new idea? For each of his topic sentences, underline the old idea with a single line. Underline the new idea with a double line. The first one has been done for you.

> *Paragraph 2: Such ambivalent feelings are now widely held toward biology.*
>
> *The phrase "ambivalent feelings" describes how people felt about physicists in the past. The phrase "are now widely held toward biology" shows that the author is comparing physics and biology and moving toward a description of how people feel about biology today.*

Paragraph 3: *As a result, several years were to pass before the full power of recombinant-DNA technology got into the hands of working scientists, who by then were itching to explore previously unattainable secrets of life.*

Paragraph 4: *The moral I draw from this painful episode is this: Never postpone experiments that have clearly defined future benefits for fear of dangers that can't be quantified.*

Paragraph 5: *Though most forms of DNA manipulation are now effectively unregulated, one important potential goal remains blocked.*

Paragraph 6: *Unlike many of my peers, I'm reluctant to accept such reasoning, again using the argument that you should never put off doing something useful for fear of evil that may never arrive.*

Paragraph 7: *If appropriate go-ahead signals come, the first resulting gene-bettered children will in no sense threaten human civilization.*

Exercise 2

The following paragraphs are from the body of an essay on genetic experimentation. The first example is in favor of genetic experimentation. The second example is against it.

In each example, the topic sentence of the second paragraph is missing. Write a new sentence for the beginning of the second paragraph. Pay attention to coherence. Include an old idea and a new idea in your new topic sentence for the second paragraph.

1. *In favor of genetic experimentation:*

   Genetic experimentation will help us live healthier lives. Gene therapies now provide new treatments for diseases, and with further experimentation we may soon be able to find cures for diseases such as cancer. Genetic manipulations have already improved some plants' resistance to plant viruses, and with further experimentation we may be able to protect children from deadly human viruses.

   _____

   _____

   Creating gene-bettered children does not mean creating a world of haves and have-nots. With genetic engineering, we will be able to control the "bad luck" genes that cause many children to be born with severe illnesses or physical limitations that have a negative impact on their, as well as their families', lives.

2. *Against genetic experimentation:*

   We cannot trust human beings to make intelligent decisions about genetic selection. Parents will want their children to be the healthiest, strongest, and most beautiful possible. Those who have the financial means will be the ones able to afford these "superbabies," while those who don't will continue to produce children with genetic defects. As a result, society will be even further divided between the haves and have-nots.

   _____

   _____

   If health insurance companies know that their clients are predisposed to certain illnesses or diseases, they may deny them coverage or charge them more money for their insurance policies. If employers have access to people's genetic information, the information could influence hiring or promotion decisions.

Write an essay on one of the numbered topics. Use ideas, vocabulary, and writing techniques from this unit. Try to incorporate the following:

- an introductory paragraph that presents the various sides of the argument and clearly states your thesis

- paragraphs (at least three) that develop your argument with supporting evidence

- a conclusion that reinforces the position you have taken. It should also end with a new idea (a warning, prediction, value judgment) that has not been mentioned before.

1. Do you favor the continuation of experimentation with human genes or do you feel that such experimentation should be limited? Take a stand and write an essay in which you express your opinion.

2. Albert Einstein said, "The right to search for truth implies also a duty; one must not conceal any part of what one has recognized to be true."

   How does Einstein's quote relate to the issue of genetic experimentation? Discuss the meaning of this quote by relating it to what you have learned about ethical issues in this unit. Conclude by stating whether you agree with Einstein's position.

UNIT 5

Sport for Sport's Sake

"I'm glad we won, and I hope that someday we'll have a
university that our football team can be proud of."

I. ANTICIPATING THE ISSUE

Discuss your answers to the questions.

1. Look at the title. Look at the cartoon. What do you think the issue of this unit will be?

2. Do you consider sports to be an important part of the academic experience? If so, how?

3. Why are college athletics so often controversial?

Read the text.

For years now, the media has covered the issue of the commercialization of sports in institutions of higher education. Many argue that college sports have become **vulgar**, even corrupt, and not deserving of the special attention they are given. Others feel that college sports continue to play an important role in the preparation of young people for real life. Why is there such disagreement?

Many academics at American universities and colleges, as well as the general public, have **dismissed** college sports as something less important than studies. They have grown tired of the **double standard** that often exists for college athletes in terms of qualifications for admission and retention. They ask why students with less-than-excellent grades and credentials are **eligible** for college admission strictly because of their athletic ability. Shouldn't all students be judged according to the same academic standards? To make matters worse, once student athletes are admitted to college, it is known that many of them are prone to taking performance-enhancing drugs, which has taken away the **prestige** that college athletes once enjoyed. Then many complain about the **hypocrisy** in admitting lower-achieving students to colleges and universities. Colleges and universities seem to be helping academically disadvantaged students by offering them scholarships to enter college, but aren't they really exploiting these students for institutional profit? Colleges may maintain their academic requirements, but there are many documented cases in which colleges have manipulated their policies to keep athletes enrolled. This is done by providing them with free tutoring or even engaging in academic **deceits** in which tutors have written the papers for athletes enrolled in English classes, performing a kind of "in-house plagiarism" to help the student-athlete make the grade.

But is the world of college athletics really so **grubby**, deserving only of criticism? Not all academics **look down their noses at** sports. In fact, many argue that without college sports, alumni would not be stimulated to come together and support their schools, often making the big contributions that are so necessary to educational institutions today. Sports **validate** the importance of college and its role in one's life after graduation. Moreover, there is sufficient evidence that athlete undergraduates graduate at the same rate as nonathlete undergraduates. For example, at Stanford University, one of the top universities in the United States, 94 percent of athletes, like nonathletes, graduate. And most importantly, many teachers and writers include sports in their **holistic** view of a young person's development. Isn't our ideal a combination of high-level physical performance and high-level performance of the mind? Hans Ulrich Gumbrecht, in his book *In Praise of Athletic Beauty*, argues that the popularity of sports can only be explained by their aesthetic appeal and that sports should be **savored** just as a beautiful work of music or art is.

Given all the controversy, it is uncertain what role sports will play in the college experience of the future. But the participants in this experience will need to weigh the financial, physical, social, and aesthetic reasons for sports' existence as they decide.

A. VOCABULARY

Look at the boldfaced words and phrases below. Try to determine their meaning from the context in the Background Reading. Cross out the word in each group that does *not* have a meaning similar to the word as it is used in the reading.

1. **vulgar**
   a. coarse
   b. uncouth
   c. mean
   d. crude

2. **dismissed**
   a. rejected
   b. given permission to leave
   c. disregarded
   d. ignored

3. **double standard**
   a. unfair arrangement
   b. wrong principle
   c. uneven rule
   d. incorrect brand

4. **eligible**
   a. competitive
   b. worthy of being chosen
   c. fit
   d. suitable

5. **prestige**
   a. importance
   b. doubt
   c. high position
   d. status

6. **hypocrisy**
   a. insincerity
   b. falsity
   c. honesty
   d. pretense

7. **deceits**
   a. candor
   b. cheating
   c. lies
   d. fraud

8. **grubby**
   a. filthy
   b. dirty
   c. nasty
   d. grueling

9. **look down their noses at**
   a. scorn
   b. praise
   c. feel superior to
   d. disdain

10. **validate**
    a. justify
    b. endorse
    c. void
    d. verify

11. **holistic**
    a. specific
    b. rounded
    c. whole
    d. broad

12. **savored**
    a. felt
    b. rejected
    c. experienced
    d. tasted

B. SUMMARIZING THE ISSUE

Work in small groups. Take notes on the negative and positive views of college sports. Summarize the issue.

1. Negative views: _____

   _____

2. Positive views: _____

   _____

3. The issue: _____

   _____

C. VALUES CLARIFICATION

Work in small groups. Discuss your answers to the questions.

1. What role do you think sports should play in college? Consider the interests of players, spectators, and alumni.

2. Do you agree more with the negative views or the positive views of college sports expressed in the Background Reading? Explain why.

III. OPINION 1: LISTENING

A. LISTENING FOR THE MAIN IDEA

Listen to the commentary. Check the statement that best summarizes the commentator's main idea.

❑ 1. The corruption of sports in college has destroyed the idea of sports.

❑ 2. Sport was never considered art because we could not preserve it.

❑ 3. Sport should be respected as much as the arts.

B. LISTENING FOR DETAILS

Listen again. Then write *T* (true) or *F* (false) for each statement. If a statement is false, change it to make it true. Compare your answers with those of another student.

_____ 1. Sport is often considered more vulgar than traditional performance activities.

_____ 2. Athletic director Gary Walters thinks sport should be given the same prestige as music.

_____ 3. Walters has a limited perspective on college sports.

_____ 4. Walters agrees that sports are a distant cousin to the arts.

_____ 5. According to commentator Frank Deford, sports have suffered because they are so sweaty.

_____ 6. Deford believes that, like athletes, artists are competitive.

_____ 7. Deford says that sports have suffered because they could not be preserved.

_____ 8. Deford thinks Michael Jordan's playing is as beautiful as Mikhail Baryshnikov's *pas de deux*[1].

_____ 9. The corruption of sports in college is a problem for Deford.

_____ 10. College athletes have been allowed to stay in college even when their academic performance was inadequate.

_____ 11. Walters believes that competition should not be a goal in college.

_____ 12. Deford thinks it makes sense that a football player cannot major in football.

_____ 13. Supporters of the arts are sometimes hypocritical, according to Deford.

_____ 14. Deford thinks that if one can bet on something, it cannot be beautiful.

---

[1]*pas de deux*: a dance for two, especially in ballet

Listen to the commentary again and circle the word you hear in each pair of underlined choices. Compare your answers with those of another student. Consider context and grammar as you check your answers.

Introduction

Here is a / the debate that shows no sign / shine of ending. The question is, should sports enjoy the same respect as the arts? Commentator Frank Deford waits / weighs in.

Commentary

Sport is not considered art. Instant, / Instead, it is variably / invariably dismissed as something lesser—even something rather more vulgar than the more / newer traditional performance activities.

Now, Gary Walters, the athletic director at Princeton, has spoken out that sport should be granted equal educational prestige with the lights / likes of drama and art and music. Isn't it / Is it time, he asks, for the educational-athletic / athlete experience on our playing fields to be accorded / recorded the same academic respect / aspect as the arts?

Walters validates his advocacy with unique credentials behind / beyond the Ivy League. He went to the Final Four as playmaker on Bill Bradley's best / last team. He was chairman of the national Division I basketball committee this year, the maestro of Mark Matches / March Madness. This is all to say that he brings the proudest / broadest perspective to college sports, and it mightily /mildly irritates Walters that sport is only considered a distant / distinct cousin to the arts.

Well, apart / up hard from simply being so sweaty, I think that sport has suffered in / suffering in comparison with the arts—or should I say, the other arts—because it is founded in / on trying to win. Artists are not so posed / supposed to be competitive. They are expected / respected to be above that. We always hear "Art for art / art's sake." Nobody ever says, "Sport for sport / sport's sake."

I also believe that sport is suffering / has suffered because, until recently, athletic performance could not be preserved. What we've / we accepted as great art—whether / well there's the book, the script, the painting, the symphony—is that which could be saved and savored. But the performances of the athletic artist / artists who ran and jumped and wrestled were gone with the win / wind.

Now, however, that we can / can't study the greys / grace of the athlete on film, a double play can be viewed as petty / pretty as any *pas de deux*. Oh / Or, please: Is not what we saw Michael Jordan do every bit / bet as artistic as what we saw Mikhail Baryshnikov do?

Of course, in the academic whirl / world, precisely that place where art is defined / the fine and certified, sport is this owned / its own worst enemy. Its / This corruption in college diminishes it so it makes it all seen / seem so grubby. But just because so many ersatz / earnest students are shoe- / show-horned into colleges as / colleges' athletes and then kept eligible academically through very indeceits / various deceits, the intrinsic essence of the athlete playing his game should not be a fact / affected.

As Walters argues, athletic competition nourishes our / are collective souls and contributes to / toward the holistic education of the total person in the same manner / matter as the arts.

Certainly / It's certain that there remains a huge double standard in college. Why can / can't a young musician major in music, a young actor major in drama, but a young football player can / can't major in football? That not only strikes me as unfair, but it encourages the hypocrisy that contributes to the situation where those hidebound defenders of the artistic faith / fame can take delight in looking down their noses at sport.

So, yes, Walters' argument makes fanfare / for fair game. Is sport one of the arts? Or, just because you can bet / bend on something, does that disqualify it as a thing of beauty?

A. READING FOR THE MAIN IDEA

Read the editorial. Check the statement that best summarizes the main idea.

❏ 1. Colleges should not focus on sports.

❏ 2. Today's student athletes do not fit into the college experience.

❏ 3. Alumni need to be stimulated to donate more money to colleges.

The Disappearing Scholar-Athlete
(Colleges Should Not Sacrifice Education to Sports)

It is the season of fat and thin envelopes, time for college admissions. This year, once again, the country's most selective liberal arts institutions will offer spots to substantial numbers of students with less than top academic **credentials** who will perform only passably in class and **segregate** themselves from other students. They are the varsity athletes brought onto campus by schools that claim both to **shun** athletic scholarships and to honor the scholar-athlete ideal. That ideal has become something of a **mockery** because the admission systems at those colleges have **lost their bearings**.

In a book published last year and in a recent follow-up for a group of New England colleges, James Shulman and William Bowen have shown in alarming detail how **out of whack** the system has become. Leave aside the many large state schools where the basketball players are effectively semi-pros, rarely and barely graduating. The problem of academically underperforming athletes exists at leafy, historic campuses like Tufts and Middlebury, where only the brightest are supposed to be accepted. Between a quarter and a third of all students at these schools now are varsity athletes, many of them recruited on numbered "coach's lists." Some are excellent students, but between half and three-quarters of male athletes end up in the bottom third of their classes at these institutions.

Yet their athletic **prowess** offers them a heavy thumb on the admission scale, much more significant than being the child of an alumnus or a member of a racial minority group. Some argue that schools are right to prize talented athletes just as they

do fine musicians or writers. But students with musical talent or those who put out the college newspaper tend to do better in school than other students. They also add to the intellectual and cultural **stew** that makes college campuses exciting. Athletes tend to segregate themselves. This was not always the case. According to the Shulman-Bowen data, varsity athletes of earlier decades did as well in school as their peers and went on to careers of community leadership.

Several colleges are sufficiently alarmed by the data to take modest action. Bowdoin, Wesleyan, Williams, and Amherst agreed last fall to reduce by between 10 and 20 percent the number of set-aside spots on coach's lists. Their fellow colleges of the 11-member New England Small College Athletic Conference say they will try to do the same in the coming year or two. And the eight members of the Ivy League, the group that includes Harvard, Yale, and Princeton, say they too will examine their athletic recruiting policies in light of the new data.

College officials say they recruit top athletes to please alumni and **spur** their donations. But the Shulman-Bowen study found that alumni favor decreasing their schools' emphasis on intercollegiate competition. Asked to rank their concerns, big **donors** consistently listed athletics toward the bottom. This is an important lesson for the colleges. Sports are wonderful and everyone likes to win, but not at the cost of sacrificing the identity and special mission of liberal arts education. ■

Originally published in *The New York Times*, April 6, 2002. Copyright ©2002 by the New York Times Company. Reprinted by permission.

B. READING FOR DETAILS

Read the questions and circle the best answer. Compare your answers with those of another student. Read the editorial again if necessary.

1. What kind of students will be offered spots in the country's most selective liberal arts institutions?
   a. those with top academic credentials
   b. those who will underperform in class
   c. those who will mix well with other students

2. What does the author think about the schools that bring varsity athletes onto campus?
   a. They shun athletic scholarships.
   b. They honor the scholar-athlete.
   c. They have lost their bearings.

3. Which problem discussed in Shulman and Bowen's book *most* concerns the author?
   a. basketball players barely graduating from large state schools
   b. underperforming athletes at historic campuses
   c. students being recruited on "coach's lists"

4. According to the author, which is most helpful for getting into college?
   a. athletic prowess
   b. being a child of an alumnus
   c. being a minority

5. Which of the following best expresses the author's view of college athletes?
   a. They should be prized like musicians or writers.
   b. They add to the intellectual and cultural stew that makes college campuses interesting.
   c. They are not as successful as the athletes of earlier decades.

6. Which college had already agreed to reduce the number of spots reserved for athletes when this article was written?
   a. Wesleyan
   b. Harvard
   c. Princeton

7. Why do college officials say they recruit top athletes?
   a. to please alumni
   b. to win
   c. to preserve the identity of the college

8. What does not concern big donors much?
   a. intercollegiate competition
   b. athletics
   c. the special mission of liberal arts education

C. WORD SEARCH

Review the boldfaced words and phrases below as they are used in the editorial. Cross out the word or phrase in each group that is *not* a synonym or does *not* have a similar meaning.

1. **credentials**	beliefs	references	qualifications
2. **segregate**	keep apart	separate	mingle
3. **shun**	seek	avoid	reject
4. **mockery**	joke	ridicule	objective
5. **lost their bearings**	became uncertain of their position	made some serious mistakes	forgot their purpose
6. **out of whack**	unfair	broken	dysfunctional
7. **prowess**	skill	dexterity	delight
8. **stew**	combination	problem	mixture
9. **spur**	motivate	stimulate	curb
10. **donors**	contributors	givers	recipients

V. SYNTHESIZING TWO OPINION PIECES

A. DISTINGUISHING OPINIONS

Work in pairs. Read each of the opinions on page 95 and decide whether it represents the view of commentator Frank Deford (Opinion 1), *The New York Times* editorial (Opinion 2), or both. Match each statement with a theme in the chart. The first one has been done for you.

THEMES	DEFORD (OPINION 1)	*THE NEW YORK TIMES* (OPINION 2)	BOTH
The art of sport			
The corruption of sports			
The academic achievement of athletes		*a*	
The value of sports to colleges and universities			

a. Varsity athletes used to be better students than they are today.

b. The grace of an athlete is as artistic as that of a dancer.

c. Sport is its own worst enemy in the academic world.

d. The role of sports in college diminishes the value of the athlete.

e. Too many athletes are allowed to stay in college in spite of their poor academic performance.

f. Sports should be granted the same prestige as drama, art, and music.

g. Athletes tend to segregate themselves from other students.

h. Schools are not right to prize talented athletes just as they do fine musicians or writers.

B. GIVING YOUR OPINION

Review the statements in Part A. Which do you agree with? Discuss your choices with a partner.

C. VOCABULARY REINFORCEMENT: Determining Meaning from Context

Read the sentences. Cross out the one word, phrase, or sentence in parentheses that does *not* make sense. Use your understanding of the boldfaced vocabulary to make your choice.

1. Because the college athlete had been using **vulgar** language during a game, (he was no longer eligible to play in the final / he could get the financial support of alumni / he added to the perception of sports as something grubby).

2. Sports are often **dismissed** by academics as (something as valuable as the arts / a subject that has gone out of whack / undeserving of being a major).

3. A **holistic** view of sports is one that takes into consideration the (breadth / bigger picture / specifics) of the athlete's talents.

4. Many people argue that there is a **double standard** in admitting athletes to top universities today. Athletes are often admitted (depending on coaches' lists / with inadequate academic credentials / because they pay more to enter college).

5. There is much **hypocrisy** surrounding the retention of athletes who are failing their courses. Student players are sometimes able to stay in college because of (grading deceits / improvements in their academic performance / papers written by tutors).

6. Some people who support the arts **look down their noses at sports.** They believe the skills of the athlete (should be savored as / are less valuable than / do not have the prestige of) those of the dancer and the artist.

7. Is it possible that student athletes **segregate** themselves because they are (shunned / mocked / validated) by other students?

8. Critics of college admission policies say that many colleges have **lost their bearings.** (They are now becoming more selective. / Their admissions criteria are not fair. / Athletics seem to have more importance than academics.)

9. The talented student athlete showed academic **prowess.** She was (spurred / encouraged / ill advised) by her professors to continue her studies.

VI. SPEAKING

A. CASE STUDY: The Gardner-Webb University Case

Read the following case that involves the breaking of ethical codes in the interest of athletics. Then work in groups to make recommendations on the case. Imagine that you are the trustees of Gardner-Webb University. You must recommend what action should be taken regarding the president's decision.

In 2000 the Gardner-Webb University men's basketball team won the NCCAA (National Christian Collegiate Athletic Association) basketball championship with the help of its senior basketball star, Carlos King, the team's leading scorer. King, named "Most Valuable Player" that year, was the cover story of the 2000 school media guide.

In 2002, it was discovered that Carlos King had received an F for cheating in his Introduction to Religion class, a course required for graduation, in the fall of 1999. At that time, he had been advised to retake the class, because, according to the Gardner-Webb policy, failing grades can be dropped when a student retakes the class and receives a passing grade. So King retook the religion class and received a D, which qualified him to play basketball in the next season.

The problem is that there is one exception to Gardner-Webb's change of grade policy: In cases of academic dishonesty, failing grades may not be removed from a student's record.

In other words, King's F should not have been removed from his record because he had been caught cheating. Thus, King should have been ineligible to continue playing basketball.

Just before the opener of the 2000 basketball season, the university's president of 16 years, Dr. Christopher White, wrote a memo to the university registrar saying "Please allow the regular repeat rule to be used regarding Mr. King's grade for Religion 202 (Fall 1999 and Summer 2000). That means that his grade for the summer school class is a normal repeat. My decision is based on my investigation into the circumstances regarding his grades."

It was not until two years after winning the 2000 championship, and only two months after the university had begun to enjoy its status in the NCCAA Division I, that it was discovered that Carlos King had not actually been eligible to play basketball during that winning season. President White responded to the breaking news by saying that King had been incorrectly advised on how he could raise his grade-point average after receiving the F. The information that his failing grade could be replaced, White said, had been given by an unnamed senior-level official. White admitted that a mistake had been made, but he claimed that the administration had "put the student's welfare first."

Many students at Gardner-Webb felt that President White had destroyed the power of the school's honor code and the integrity of the university, and called for White's resignation; one student explained that he had purposely chosen to attend Gardner-Webb for its Christian ethics and believed he could no longer attend the university, because of this scandal. Faculty members protested by canceling classes and removing the honor code plaque from their classroom walls. The scandal tore the university community apart. For example, eight faculty members and administrators were fired, demoted, or chose to resign in protest.

After a 10-hour meeting on September 22, 2002, the school's trustees reaffirmed Christopher White's presidency. The chairman said his board did not believe the president should be removed for a mistake made two years earlier. Under White's presidency, the university's endowment had been increased to $28 million from $4 million. During his tenure, White had been able to raise the university's profile and attract more qualified students. Although some trustees agreed that White should step down, more of them felt that he should be pardoned. University alumni wrote a petition asking faculty members to reconsider their resignations and the university to reinstate demoted deans.

However, many people felt that the president could no longer represent the core values of the university. One student said, "If he's humble at all, he should resign."

B. DISCUSSION QUESTIONS

Work in groups. Discuss your answers to the questions.

1. Do you believe, as Frank Deford does, that "sport is art"? Has athletic performance suffered unfairly because it is competitive or, until recently, could not be preserved? Are you in favor of or against granting sport the same academic respect as the arts?

2. How should college admissions for athletes be dealt with? Should special spots be reserved for them?

A. GRAMMAR: Use of the Passive Voice

Notice Notice the verb forms in the following sentences from the commentary and editorial. Discuss your answers to the questions below.

> a. *Sport is not considered art. Instead, it **is** invariably **dismissed** as something lesser— even something rather more vulgar than the more traditional performance activities.*
>
> b. *As Walters argues, athletic competition **nourishes** our collective souls and **contributes** to the holistic education of the total person in the same manner as the arts.*
>
> c. *They are the varsity athletes **brought** onto campus by schools that claim both to shun athletic scholarships and to honor the scholar-athlete ideal.*

1. Which verbs are expressed in the passive voice? Which verbs are expressed in the active voice?

2. Does the reader know the agent in each sentence? If so, what is it? Who or what is responsible for what the verb expresses?

3. Why do writers sometimes choose to use the passive voice rather than the active voice?

Explanation The passive voice is commonly used in objective writing. We use the passive when we want to focus on *the thing being done* or *the process being described* more than on the agent—the person or thing that causes something. The passive is frequently used in academic, scientific, and journalistic writing.

When we want to avoid mentioning or do not know who is responsible for what is done, we use the passive voice. The passive can help writers avoid "pointing a finger" or blaming anyone in particular for a result.

Sentence *c* comes from a passive structure, and the agent is mentioned with the *by* phrase. If this sentence were written in the active voice, it would place more emphasis on the agent (schools) and less on the receiver (varsity athletes):

> *Schools that claim both to shun athletic scholarships and to honor the scholar-athlete ideal bring the varsity athletes onto campus.*

Sentence *a* is also written in the passive voice, but the agent is not mentioned. Notice how the meaning would change in Sentence *a* if commentator Frank Deford had used the active voice and supplied an agent. Emphasis would then be placed on those responsible (academics) rather than the thing being done (considering sports, dismissing sports):

> *Academics do not consider sport to be art. Instead, they dismiss it as something lesser—even something rather more vulgar than the more traditional performance activities.*

Exercise

Read the following passive sentences from Deford's commentary. Underline the passive structure(s) in each sentence. Rewrite them in the active voice. You will have to supply an agent in each case. Then work with a partner to discuss how the meaning changes when the sentences are rewritten. Why did the commentator choose to use the passive voice in all of these sentences?

1. Now, Gary Walters, the athletic director at Princeton, has spoken out that sport should be granted equal educational prestige with the likes of drama and art and music.

   _____

   _____

2. Is it time, he asks, for the educational-athletic experience on our playing fields to be accorded the same academic respect as the arts?

   _____

   _____

3. This is to say that he brings the broadest perspective to college sports, and it mightily irritates Walters that sport is only considered a distant cousin to the arts.

   _____

   _____

4. Well, apart from being so sweaty, I think that sport has suffered in comparison with the arts—or should I say, the other arts—because it is founded on trying to win.

   _____

   _____

5. They [artists] are expected to be above that.

   _____

   _____

6. I also believe that sport has suffered because, until recently, athletic performance could not be preserved.

   _____

   _____

7. What we accepted as great art—whether the book, the script, the painting, or the symphony—is that which could be saved and savored.

_____

_____

8. Now, however, that we can study the grace of the athlete on film, a double play can be viewed as pretty as any *pas de deux*.

_____

_____

9. But because so many ersatz students are shoe-horned into colleges as athletes and then kept eligible academically through various deceits, the intrinsic essence of the athlete playing his game should not be affected.

_____

_____

B. WRITING STYLE: Argument

Notice Notice the style of writing used by both the commentator and the editorial writer. Even though they have opposite views on the role of sports in college, both use similar techniques to build their arguments. What are these techniques?

Explanation Both writers use argument to convince listeners and readers to agree with their point of view. Argumentative writing tries to persuade us by appealing to logic and reason.

There are generally four ways to do this: Writers can use *statistics* such as numbers, opinion polls, or data to support a claim. They may use *factual details and examples* such as names, places, and events as a helpful reference to their point of view. Another technique is to make an *appeal to authority*, or a reference to the "experts," as a support for an opinion. Finally, writers sometimes use *personal testimony*, or their own experience, when it is appropriate and persuasive.

Exercise

Refer to Deford's commentary and *The New York Times* article. Which of the techniques described above are used to argue the positions on sports in college? Take notes to list examples of each type used in Opinion 1 and Opinion 2. Compare your examples with those of another student.

Deford's Commentary / Opinion 1 (pages 90-91)

    1. Statistics: _____

    _____

    2. Factual details and examples: _____

    _____

    3. Appeal to authority: _____

    _____

    4. Personal testimony: _____

    _____

The New York Times Editorial / Opinion 2 (page 92)

    1. Statistics: _____

    _____

    2. Factual details and examples: _____

    _____

    3. Appeal to authority: _____

    _____

    4. Personal testimony: _____

    _____

C. ESSAY QUESTIONS

Write an essay on one of the numbered topics. Use ideas, vocabulary, and writing techniques from this unit. Try to incorporate the following:

- an introductory paragraph that presents both sides of the argument and clearly states your thesis
- body paragraphs (at least three) that develop your argument with supporting evidence
- a conclusion that reinforces the position you have taken and ends with a new idea (a warning, prediction, or value judgment) that has not been mentioned earlier in the essay

1. Read the following quote.

   > It may therefore be worth a self-critical thought whether we intellectuals who want to pay exclusive attention to the concerns of the mind have not entered a hidden alliance with the type of consumerism that tries to convince society that a life glued to the computer screen and the cellular phone—a life in which body and space have become negligible dimensions—is the most fulfilling life. That is why I believe it matters, more than ever before perhaps, that we keep open the possibility for events where physical intensity and intellectual intensity can come together—that we keep such occasions open for those among our students who want to perform music, create art, and play sports, as well as for their readers, listeners, and spectators. We will lose much more than a political edge if we allow the next generation to believe that a fusion of software and critical spirit is the formula for a desirable life.
   > (Hans Ulrich Gumbrecht, Professor of Comparative Literature, Stanford University)

   What is Gumbrecht saying about the value of sports? Do you agree with him? Write an essay in which you express your opinion.

2. Compare and contrast the attitudes toward collegiate sports in your country with those in the United States. Use the ideas expressed in this unit to make your comparison.

Drawing the Line on Immigration

"Well, they look pretty undocumented to me."

I. ANTICIPATING THE ISSUE

Discuss your answers to the questions.

1. Look at the title. Look at the cartoon. What do you think the issue of this unit will be?

2. What do you know about the situation of undocumented workers in the United States or other countries?

3. Do you think that law officials should crack down on illegal immigrants, or do you think that opportunities should be made to allow them to become citizens?

Read the text.

Although the United States is recognized as "an immigrant nation," there continues to be strong disagreement over who has the right to immigrate into the country and who does not. A debate has been **spawned** over whether more undocumented workers should be allowed to cross national borders and start a new life in the United States.

Some people support giving legal status to those illegal immigrants already living in the United States. They are sympathetic toward the estimated 12 million illegal immigrants who have already established their lives and families in the country. In fact, many of these families are a mix of Americans by birth, permanent residents, and undocumented workers. Although these undocumented workers have raised their children as Americans and have already **assimilated** into American culture, they are still not viewed as true citizens because they did not come to the country legally. If these people were sent back to their countries, their families would be split up. Furthermore, those who support illegal immigrants point out that illegal workers do many of the jobs that Americans will not do: pick crops on farms, clean houses and office buildings, wash dishes in restaurants, and take care of people's children. Finally, those who support legal status for illegal immigrants often comment that most Americans come from families of immigrants who came to the United States when immigration policies were more open. Why, they ask, should today's immigrants be treated so differently?

Others view the **exodus** of foreigners to the United States as a threat, especially as more and more illegal immigrants cross the U.S.-Mexico border. They see immigrants as an **invasion** of less educated people. They also point out that the hiring of illegal workers brings down the money-making power of lower-income Americans; as more and more illegal immigrants take on American jobs at lower wages, salaries go down. Moreover, with more illegal immigrants living and having children in the United States, Americans must spend more of their tax dollars on social services. In addition, supporters of this view call attention to the problems of crime, saying that the United States needs to better **patrol** its borders, that not enough money is put into security. Too many drug **smugglers** are able to cross borders, and open borders encourage powerful drug **cartels** to enter and operate in the United States. Also, many illegal aliens are being smuggled into the country as **human cargo**. All this criminal activity hurts the **tranquility** of this nation. Those who oppose giving legal status to illegal immigrants say that the American dream continues to exist but only for those who are not American.

The problem of illegal immigration is **multifaceted**. It affects the nation's economy, political system, and national identity. It is also **unprecedented**. Never before have so many illegal immigrants been able to cross borders and find work so easily in the United States. The debate over illegal immigration is really about how people see America as a **sovereign** nation: as a country that is strong because of its immigrants from other nations, or as a country that is strong because of its independence from other nations.

A. VOCABULARY

The following sentences are from the Background Reading. Try to determine the meaning of each boldfaced word or phrase. Write a synonym or your own definition for each of the boldfaced words.

1. A debate has been **spawned** over whether more undocumented immigrants should be allowed to cross national borders and start a new life in the United States.

   _____

2. Although these undocumented workers have raised their children as Americans and **assimilated** into American culture, they are still not viewed as true citizens.

   _____

3. Others view the **exodus** of foreigners as a threat, especially as more and more illegal immigrants cross the U.S.-Mexico border.

   _____

4. They see immigrants as an **invasion** of less educated people.

   _____

5. They also point out the problems of crime, saying that the United States needs to better **patrol** its borders, that not enough money is put into security.

   _____

6. Too many drug **smugglers** are able to cross these borders . . . many illegal aliens are being smuggled into the country as human cargo.

   _____

7. The open border encourages powerful drug **cartels** to enter and operate in the United States.

   _____

8. Also many illegal aliens are being smuggled into the country as **human cargo**.

   _____

9. All this criminal activity hurts the **tranquility** of this nation.

   _____

10. The problem of illegal immigration is **multifaceted**. It affects the nation's economy, political system, and national identity.

_____

11. It is also **unprecedented**. Never before have so many illegal immigrants been able to cross borders and find work in the United States.

_____

12. The debate over illegal immigration is really about how people see America as a **sovereign** nation: as a country that is strong because of its immigrants from other nations, or as a country that is strong because of its independence from other nations.

_____

B. SUMMARIZING THE ISSUE

Work in small groups. Take notes on the following points from the Background Reading. Summarize the issue.

1. The issue (*state in your own words*): _____

_____

_____

2. Proponents' (of supporting illegal immigrants) arguments: _____

_____

3. Opponents' (of supporting illegal immigrants) arguments: _____

_____

C. VALUES CLARIFICATION

Work in small groups. Discuss your answers to the questions.

1. What is your reaction to the U.S.-Mexico border issue? What do you think should be done about it?

2. Is there a difference between the first immigrants to the United States and those of today? How should people who cross borders and find jobs as undocumented workers in the United States be viewed?

A. LISTENING FOR THE MAIN IDEAS

Listen to the commentary. Check the statement that best summarizes the commentator's main idea.

❑ 1. The border between the United States and Mexico is a dump that needs to be cleaned up.

❑ 2. The U.S. government needs to work harder to enforce immigration laws.

❑ 3. We need a stronger barrier between the United States and Mexico to prevent illegal immigrants from crossing the border.

B. LISTENING FOR DETAILS

Read the questions and answers. Listen to the commentary again and circle the best answer to each question. Compare your answers with those of another student. Listen again if necessary.

1. Who does commentator Jim Gilchrist try to organize in order to deal with the immigration problem?
   a. the Senate
   b. the Minutemen
   c. civilians

2. What has Jim Gilchrist changed his mind about?
   a. a wall along the border
   b. the Mexicans
   c. illegal immigration

3. About how far does the U.S.-Mexico border stretch?
   a. 2,000 miles
   b. 12,000 miles
   c. 20,000 miles

4. What kind of terrain does the U.S.-Mexico border cross?
   a. arid desert
   b. green valleys
   c. grassy mountains

5. Which of the following describes the dividing line?
   a. A 13-foot-wide road parallels it.
   b. It is made of 40-foot-high barbed-wire fence.
   c. There are heaps of trash on both sides.

6. Which best describes Gilchrist's attitude toward having a physical barrier to prevent illegal immigration?
    a. He thinks the U.S. government will not support it.
    b. He thinks it is the only solution.
    c. He thinks it is one of many solutions.

7. Which of the following physically describes the barrier Gilchrist wants?
    a. It is 2,000 miles long.
    b. It has steel walls.
    c. It is 50 feet high.

8. What would Gilchrist add to a barrier?
    a. border patrol agents
    b. solar devices
    c. underground tunnels

9. What would *not* happen after building a barrier?
    a. Rubbish would disappear.
    b. Wildlife would die.
    c. Vegetation would return.

10. What would this physical barrier represent?
    a. It would represent the United States as a sovereign nation.
    b. It would represent the United States's domestic tranquility.
    c. It would represent the United States's failure to stop illegal immigration.

11. What fear does Gilchrist have about illegal immigrants?
    a. They will overthrow the government.
    b. They will threaten our economic status.
    c. They will assimilate with Americans.

C. TEXT COMPLETION AND DISCRETE LISTENING

Read the commentary. For each blank, write *a*, *an*, or *the*, or *X* if there is no article needed. Use the context and your knowledge of grammar to decide where articles are necessary. Then listen to the commentary to check your answers.

Introduction

The trouble _____ Senate has had with an immigration deal is not _____
            1   2
surprise to commentator Jim Gilchrist. He's the founder of _____ Minuteman
                                                            3
Project. It's had a lot of attention in the last year for organizing _____ civilians
                                                                      4
to patrol the border between the U.S. and Mexico.

He says that until _____ couple of months ago, he opposed building a wall
5
along _____ entire Mexican border. Now Jim Gilchrist has changed his mind.
6
He says he's lost confidence in lawmakers' ability to come up with _____
7
better solution to the problem of illegal immigration.

Commentary

The U.S.-Mexico border is 1,989 miles from San Diego, California to Brownsville,
Texas. It's covered by a web of well-trodden trails, carved out by _____
8
smugglers of drug and human cargo. It goes through desert highlands, mountain
ranges and valleys of arid, sparsely vegetated desert, and grassy plains.

Gusts of wind whip up the air into _____ choking yellow dust. Most of
9
the way, _____ 30-foot-wide dirt road parallels a worn 4-foot-high barbed-
10
wire fence. That's _____ legal dividing line between the United States and
11
Mexico. Heaps of trash litter the ground on _____ both sides of the border.
12
Plastic bottles and jugs, _____ clothing, backpacks, rusted cans that once held
13
food. The border is _____ international public dump for the endless exodus of
14
people coming north. _____ border area appears as an unguarded, lawless
15
wasteland of treacherous mountains and deserts, _____ open invitation to
16
enter at will for illegal aliens and criminal cartels.

I have no confidence that the U.S. government has any intention of bringing
the United States back under the rule of law insofar as immigration laws are
concerned. I think that _____ physical barrier separating the United States
17
and Mexico is now an appealing component of _____ multi-faceted solution
18
to the invasion of the United States

We need a 2,000-mile-long physical barrier from San Diego, California, to
Brownsville, Texas. It would include _____ dual concrete and steel-reinforced
19

walls 15 feet high and 10 feet deep into the ground. There would be _____ 20 60-foot-wide dirt road between them.

Stationary and mobile towers, staffed with border patrol agents, would provide _____ series of observation posts. High-tech video and sensor devices would 21 be employed to detect any intrusion into _____ area between the dual walls, 22 and _____ sonar devices would randomly check for underground tunneling. 23

After the walls are erected, _____ healing process for nature would begin. 24 Eventually, _____ millions of pounds of rubbish would be manually cleared. 25 Wildlife and vegetation would spawn and return the areas to their natural habitat.

The 2,000-mile physical barrier would be _____ last resort for us to survive 26 as a sovereign nation, our nation's final attempt to preserve its prosperity and domestic tranquility. And sadly, it would stand as _____ constant reminder of 27 the failure of America's political and business leaders to stop _____ invasion of 28 a magnitude unprecedented in _____ history of the United States. _____ 29 30 invasion that threatens our heritage, culture, prosperity, domestic tranquility, governance under the rule of law and our very existence as _____ sovereign 31 nation of assimilated Americans.

IV. OPINION 2: READING

A. READING FOR THE MAIN IDEA

Read the editorial on the next page. Check the statement that best summarizes the author's main idea.

❑ 1. Ángel Espinoza and the author's grandfather should have the same rights because they both worked hard to become American citizens.

❑ 2. Espinoza should not have the same rights as the author's grandfather because he crossed the border illegally.

❑ 3. The case of Espinoza should be viewed differently than the case of the author's grandfather because of the times in which they lived.

Ángels in America

by John Tierney

CHICAGO—Ángel Espinoza doesn't understand why Republicans on **Capitol Hill** are determined to **deport** Mexicans like him. I don't get it either. He makes me think of my Irish grandfather.

They both left farms and went to the South Side of Chicago, arriving with relatively little education. My grandfather took a job in the stockyards and lived in an Irish boardinghouse nearby. Espinoza started as a dishwasher and lived with his brother in a Mexican neighborhood.

Like my grandfather, who became a streetcar motorman and then a police officer, Espinoza moved on to better-paying jobs and a better home of his own. Like my grandfather, Espinoza married an American-born descendant of immigrants from his native country.

But whereas my grandfather became a citizen, Espinoza couldn't even become a legal resident. Once he married an American, he applied, but was rejected because he'd once been caught at the border and sent home with an order to stay out. Violating that order made him **ineligible** for a green card and eligible for deportation.

"I had to tell my 4-year-old daughter that one day I might not come home," he said. "I work hard and pay taxes and don't want any welfare. Why deport me?"

The official answer, of course, is that he **violated** the law. My grandfather didn't. But my grandfather didn't have to. There weren't **quotas** on Europeans or most other immigrants in 1911, even though, relative to the population, there were more immigrants arriving and living here than there are today. If America could **absorb** my grandfather, why keep out Espinoza?

It's been argued that Mexicans are different from past immigrants because they're closer to home and less likely to **assimilate**. Compared with other immigrants today, they're less educated, and their children are more likely to get poor grades and drop out of school. Therefore, the argument goes, Mexicans are in danger of becoming an underclass living in linguistically isolated **ghettos**.

Those concerns sound reasonable in theory. But if you look at studies of immigrants, you find that the typical story is much more like Espinoza's. He dropped out of school at age 16 in southern Mexico, when his family needed money for medical bills. He paid a **coyote** to sneak him across the border and went to the Mexican neighborhood of Pilsen in Chicago, a metropolitan area that is now home to the second-largest Mexican population in the nation.

Espinoza started off making less than $4 an hour as a dishwasher in a restaurant that **flouted** the minimum-wage law. But he became a cook and worked up to $15 an hour. He switched to driving a street-cleaning truck, a job that now pays him $17 an hour, minus taxes and Social Security.

By age 24, he and his wife, Anita, had saved enough to buy a house for about $200,000 in Villa Park, a suburb where most people don't speak Spanish. Now 27, Espinoza's still working on his English (we spoke in Spanish), but his daughter is already speaking English at her preschool.

There's nothing unusual about his progress. More than half of the Mexican immigrants in Chicago own their own homes, and many are moving to the suburbs. No matter where they live, their children learn English.

You can hear this on the sidewalks and school corridors in Mexican neighborhoods like Pilsen, where most teenagers speak to one another in English. A national survey by the Pew Hispanic Center found that nearly all **second-generation** Latinos are either bilingual or English-dominant, and by the next generation 80 percent are English-dominant and virtually none speak just Spanish.

Yesterday, the Senate seemed close to a deal letting most immigrants become legal residents. But it fell apart when Republicans fought to add restrictions, including some that could prevent an immigrant with Espinoza's history from qualifying.

Bobby Rush, a Democratic representative from Chicago, is trying to pass protections for the Espinozas and other families in danger of being separated. The issue has **galvanized** other Chicago public officials and immigrant advocates, who are planning to take the families to Washington to press their case.

I'd like to see Republicans on Capitol Hill explain to Espinoza why he's less deserving than their immigrant ancestors, but that's probably too much to expect. Espinoza has a simpler wish: "I would like them to tell my American daughter why her father can't stay with her." ∎

B. READING FOR DETAILS

Circle the letter that best completes each sentence, according to the author's opinion. Compare your answers with those of another student. Read the article again if necessary.

1. Ángel Espinoza _____.
   a. is supported by Republicans
   b. is Mexican
   c. has an Irish grandfather

2. Both Ángel and the author's grandfather _____.
   a. lived in Chicago
   b. lived in boardinghouses
   c. worked as dishwashers

3. A significant difference between Ángel and the author's grandfather is that they did not both _____.
   a. move on to better-paying jobs
   b. marry an American
   c. become citizens

4. The reason why Espinoza could not become a legal resident was that he _____.
   a. was caught crossing the border
   b. was deported
   c. has a daughter in the United States

5. The author's grandfather did not violate the law because _____.
   a. he was part of a quota
   b. he arrived in 1911
   c. he was already living in the United States

6. Some argue that Mexicans are different from past immigrants because they are _____.
   a. less likely to integrate
   b. better educated
   c. from ghettos

7. The author _____.
   a. agrees that Mexicans will not assimilate
   b. admires Mexicans for their hard work
   c. thinks the Mexican population is growing too fast

8. The wage that Espinoza earned at the restaurant was _____.
   a. minimum wage
   b. $15 an hour
   c. $17 an hour

9. Espinoza has _____.
   a. a wife who does not speak Spanish
   b. a house that cost $200,000
   c. a daughter entering preschool

10. Most Mexican immigrants _____.
   a. cannot afford to buy their own homes
   b. are moving to the suburbs
   c. have children who learn English

11. Most second-generation Latinos _____.
   a. are bilingual
   b. only speak English
   c. only speak Spanish

12. The group most interested in allowing immigrants to become legal residents is _____.
   a. the Senate
   b. the Republicans
   c. the Democrats

13. When the author examines Espinoza's case, he feels _____.
   a. confused
   b. angry
   c. sympathetic

C. WORD SEARCH

The following words and phrases have more than one definition in the dictionary. Choose the correct definition based on the context of the words in the editorial "Ángels in America."

1. **Capitol Hill**
   a. a hill in Washington, D.C.
   b. the U.S. Congress

2. **deport**
   a. to expel from a country
   b. to behave or conduct (oneself) in a given manner

3. **ineligible**
   a. disqualified by law, rule, or provision
   b. unworthy of being chosen; unfit

4. **violated**
   a. broke
   b. raped or sexually abused someone

5. **quota**
   a. a number or percentage, especially of people, constituting or designated as an upper limit
   b. a number or percentage, especially of people, constituting a required or targeted minimum

6. **absorb**
   a. reduce or lessen something
   b. receive or take something in as part of oneself or itself

7. **assimilate**
   a. to incorporate and absorb into the mind
   b. to become similar; come to resemble

8. **ghettos**
   a. sections of a city occupied by a minority group who live there, especially because of social, economic, or legal pressure
   b. walled quarters in a European city to which Jews were restricted beginning in the Middle Ages

9. **coyote**
   a. a small, wolf-like, carnivorous animal
   b. a person who smuggles illegal immigrants into the United States, especially across the Mexican border

10. **flouted**
    a. laughed at with contempt and derision
    b. showed contempt for; scorned

11. **second-generation**
    a. of or relating to a person or persons whose parents are immigrants
    b. of, relating to, or being the second form or version available to users

12. **galvanized**
    a. coated with rust-resistant zinc
    b. aroused to awareness or action; spurred

A. DISTINGUISHING OPINIONS

Authors can have different viewpoints, but their opinions can sometimes be similar. Review the commentary and the editorial. Work in groups. Discuss whether Gilchrist and / or Tierney would agree with the statements below. Put the statements in Gilchrist's circle or Tierney's circle. If you think they would both agree, put the statement in the intersection of the circles.

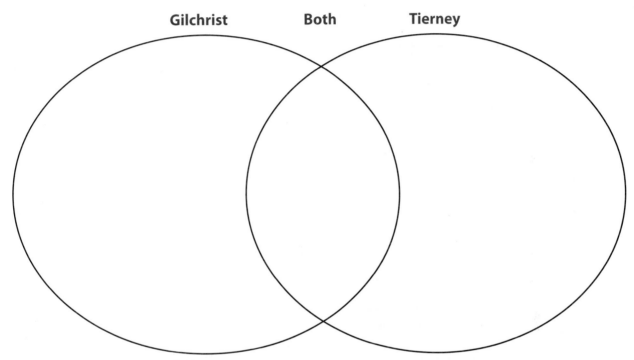

Gilchrist   Both   Tierney

a. An immigrant who is caught at the border should be deported.

b. There should be quotas on immigrants coming into the United States.

c. The U.S. government has not done enough to solve the immigration problem.

d. Most Mexican immigrants who cross the border illegally are searching for prosperity.

e. Many Mexican immigrants may not assimilate as easily as past immigrants.

f. Mexican immigrants tend to work hard to get ahead.

B. GIVING YOUR OPINION

Give your own opinions on the statements in Part A. Discuss them with the other students in your group.

C. VOCABULARY REINFORCEMENT: Word Forms

Work in small groups. Fill in the missing word forms for each vocabulary item in the chart. (An *X* has been placed in the box if there is no related word form.) Use a dictionary if necessary.

NOUNS	VERBS	ADJECTIVES
	deport	
	violate	
	absorb	
	assimilate	
X	galvanize	
	patrol	
	X	ineligible
	litter	
invasion		
tranquility		

Complete the sentences with the correct word from the chart. There may be more than one correct answer.

1. Espinoza's _____ for a green card is due to the fact that he'd once been caught at the border and sent back to Mexico.

2. The government has been unable to handle the _____ of illegal immigrants because it is so difficult to find them and so costly to send them home.

3. Many illegal immigrants are able to cross the U.S.-Mexico border because

   it is so poorly _____.

4. American citizens are divided over immigration issues. Some see illegal immigrant workers as necessary for maintaining the economy; others think

   they should be _____.

5. With 12 million illegal immigrants already living in the United States, can the country still _____ any new arrivals?

6. It is often pointed out that earlier immigrants were forced to _____ with Americans more quickly than they are today because they had to learn English upon their arrival.

7. Some argue that illegal immigrants should not be allowed to become legal because they _____ the law by crossing borders.

8. Many immigrants have come to the United States in search of a more _____ life, leaving war and discrimination behind them.

9. When they heard that the government was planning to send illegal immigrants back to their countries, immigrant communities were _____ to demonstrate against the proposal.

10. Espinoza left his first neighborhood, covered with _____, and moved into a middle-class suburb outside of Chicago.

VI. SPEAKING

A. CASE STUDY: Should Illegal Immigrants Be Granted Amnesty?

The following reading presents a true case that raises the issue of illegal immigration. Study the case, then follow the procedures for the debate.

Raymundo, an illegal alien, lives a secret life. He is more worried than ever about being deported—so much so that the skin under his chin sometimes breaks out in red spots. When rumors circulate of immigration raids in Homestead, Florida, where he lives, he refuses to leave the house. At his handyman job in the Florida Keys, he monitors the radio constantly for reports of Cuban refugees washing up on shore, knowing the highways will soon be full of law enforcement. He's panicked about what to do when his driver's license expires; new rules require that he show proof of legal residency to renew it. "I try not to think about it all," says Raymundo, 28. But the fear of being caught worries him constantly.

Raymundo is planning to marry a legal immigrant, but he is not sure that this will legalize his status. Over dinner one night last week, his family members, some of whom are legal residents, pointed to Raymundo's shaved head. "You look like a gang member," one of them said, concerned that he'd be a target of increased gang raids by authorities. "Don't worry," he replied, assuring her that he wears his work cap whenever he goes out.

(continued)

The Debate

Divide into two groups for a debate. The debate will focus on whether illegal immigrants should be granted amnesty, the act of an authority (such as a government) by which pardon is granted to a large group of individuals. Use the information in the case to help you plan your arguments.

The Teams

1. **Team A:** You are in favor of amnesty for illegal immigrants. You believe that amnesty is the best policy for dealing with the illegal immigrants already living and working in the United States. You support helping these people work toward becoming legal residents in the United States.

2. **Team B:** You are against amnesty for illegal immigrants. You believe that illegal immigrants have violated the law and should be deported. You think allowing them to stay and work toward becoming legal residents of the United States sends the wrong message.

The Procedure

1. Teams A and B prepare their arguments in small groups, citing evidence from the case and the readings.

2. Teams A and B face each other for a debate.

3. Team A begins with a one-minute presentation.

4. Continue in this fashion. A member of a team is not allowed to speak until someone from the opposite team has made a counterargument.

After the debate, the moderator evaluates the strength of both arguments.

B. DISCUSSION QUESTIONS

Work in groups. Discuss your answers to the questions.

1. Do you agree with Jim Gilchrist that we need to build stronger borders and keep more immigrants from coming into the United States? Is this the best solution to controlling illegal immigration? Is it one of many solutions?

2. Do you support John Tierney's opinion that we should support the illegal immigrants who are already residing and working in the country? Should they be offered the same opportunities past immigrants have had?

A. GRAMMAR: Comparisons

Notice Notice the structure of the sentences from the editorial. What is being compared? What is being contrasted?

1. They **both** left farms and went to the south side of Chicago, arriving with relatively little education.

2. **Like** my grandfather, who became a streetcar motorman and then a police officer, Espinoza moved on to better-paying jobs and a better home of his own. **Like** my grandfather, Espinoza married an American-born descendent of immigrants from his native country.

3. But **whereas** my grandfather became a citizen, Espinoza couldn't even become a legal resident.

4. It's been argued that Mexicans **are different from** past immigrants because they're **closer** to home and **less likely** to assimilate.

5. **Compared with** other immigrants today, they're **less educated**, and their children are **more likely** to get poor grades and drop out of school.

Explanation Tierney uses a variety of comparison / contrast structures to compare Espinoza with his grandfather and Mexican immigrants with other immigrants. He shows similarities in sentences 1 and 2. He shows differences in sentences 3 through 5.

There are several ways to present comparison / contrast.

Prepositional phrases: Prepositional phrases can be used for comparison / contrast. Use these to introduce noun phrases:

Comparison	**Contrast**
like X, Y . . .	*unlike X, Y . . .*
similar to X, Y . . .	*different from X, Y . . .*
in addition to X, Y . . .	*instead of X, Y . . .*
	compared with X, Y . . .
	in spite of X, Y . . .
	despite X, Y . . .

For example:

Like my grandfather, Espinoza married an American-born descendent of immigrants from his native country.

(continued)

Transitions: Transitions can be used to introduce comparison / contrast. Use these to connect two independent clauses:

Comparison

Similarly
In the same way
Likewise
In like manner

Contrast

In contrast
On the other hand
Nevertheless
Conversely

For example:

*Most early immigrants to the United States came from European countries; **conversely**, many of today's immigrants come from Latin American countries.*

Subordinating Conjunctions: Subordinating conjunctions can be used to introduce adverbial clauses of contrast:

Contrast

whereas
while
although
even though

For example:

*But **whereas** my grandfather became a citizen, Espinoza couldn't even become a legal resident.*

Exercise

Combine the sentences to show comparison and contrast. Use the word or phrase in parentheses to combine the ideas. Change sentence structure when necessary.

1. A couple of months ago, Gilchrist opposed building a wall along the entire Mexican border. Gilchrist now thinks a physical barrier is necessary. (although)

   _____

   _____

2. The Mexican side of the border has heaps of trash that litter the ground. The U.S. side of the border has heaps of trash that litter the ground, too. (like)

   _____

   _____

3. Plastic bottles and jugs, backpacks, and rusted cans are now dumped along the border. Wildlife and vegetation would spawn after erecting the walls there. (nevertheless)

_____

_____

4. Jim Gilchrist feels that illegal immigrants from Mexico should be prevented from invading the United States. John Tierney feels Mexicans should be absorbed into the United States just as his father was. (compared with)

_____

_____

5. Ángel Espinoza got better paying jobs and married an American-born descendant. Tierney's grandfather got better paying jobs and married an American-born descendant, too. (both)

_____

_____

6. Espinoza may not qualify for becoming a legal resident. Espinoza has lived in the United States for 12 years, saved enough money to buy a house, and is learning English. (even though)

_____

_____

7. Most Mexican teenagers speak to one another in English. Most second-generation Latinos are either bilingual or English-dominant. (likewise)

_____

_____

8. Some Republicans are fighting to restrict immigrants like Espinoza from qualifying as legal residents. Democrats are trying to pass protections for immigrants like Espinoza. (on the other hand)

_____

_____

9. Many past immigrants were forced into an underclass and to live in ghettos. Many immigrants today start out living in poorer, linguistically isolated neighborhoods. (in the same way)

_____

_____

10. Gilchrist would like to see the government do a better job of stopping the invasion of immigrants into the country. Tierney feels the government should find a way to let most immigrants become legal residents. (whereas)

_____

_____

B. WRITING STYLE: Comparison / Contrast Essays

Notice Reread paragraphs 2 through 4 of "Ángels in America." Which paragraph(s) illustrate a comparison between the author's grandfather and Espinoza? Which paragraph(s) illustrate a contrast between the author's grandfather and Espinoza? Does the author seem to be more interested in drawing similarities or citing differences between his grandfather and Espinoza

Explanation The editorial "Ángels in America" is not organized as a comparison / contrast essay. However, paragraphs 2 through 4 represent the way the body of a comparison / contrast essay might be organized. In paragraphs 2 and 3, the author focuses on the similarities between his grandfather and Espinoza; in paragraph 4, he points out the differences. The author gives more weight to the similarities than to the differences of immigrants in the past and those of the present.

The ideas in these three paragraphs could be organized into a comparison / contrast essay. There are two basic patterns of comparison / contrast essays. Both should include a thesis statement that makes it clear whether comparisons or contrasts are more important. Consider the ideas in "Ángels in America" organized by each of the following methods.

Point-by-Point Method

This is the method used in the three paragraphs in "Ángels in America." In this method, each point is discussed in relation to the two topics being compared or contrasted: Espinoza and the author's grandfather. This method is usually easier for the reader to understand in a longer essay because comparisons are made throughout the essay.

Thesis statement: The experience of today's immigrants to the United States is not so different from the experience of immigrants to the country in the early 1900s.

I. Move from farm to Chicago (comparison)
   A. Grandfather
      1. Took a job in the stockyards and lived in an Irish boardinghouse nearby
   B. Espinoza
      1. Started as a dishwasher and lived with his brother in a Mexican neighborhood

II. Move up in the world (comparison)
   A. Grandfather
      1. From a streetcar motorman to a police officer
      2. Married an American-born descendant of immigrants from his native country
   B. Espinoza
      1. On to a better-paying job
      2. Bought a home of his own
      3. Married an American-born descendant of immigrants from his native country

III. Attaining citizenship (contrast)
   A. Grandfather
      1. Became a citizen
   B. Espinoza
      1. Could not become a legal resident
         a. Rejected because he had once been caught at the border
         b. Ineligible for green card
         c. Eligible for deportation

Block Method

In this method of comparison / contrast, each topic is discussed separately. In this case, the topics are the grandfather and Espinoza. This method is usually easier for the writer but more difficult for the reader because the comparisons are not made clear until the second part of the body of the essay.

Thesis statement: The experience of today's immigrants to the United States is not so different from the experience of immigrants to the country in the early 1900s.

I. Grandfather
   A. Left farm and went to south-side Chicago with little education
      1. Took a job in the stockyards and lived in an Irish boardinghouse nearby
   B. Moved up in the world
      1. From a streetcar motorman to a police officer
      2. Married an American-born descendant of immigrants from his native country
   C. Became a citizen

II. Espinoza
   A. Left farm and went to south-side Chicago with little education
      1. Started as a dishwasher and lived with his brother in a Mexican neighborhood
   B. Moved up in the world
      1. On to a better-paying job
      2. Bought a home of his own
      3. Married an American-born descendant of immigrants from his native country
   C. Could not become a legal resident

Exercise

Consider the views of Gilchrist and Tierney concerning illegal immigration. Choose three points to discuss in a comparison / contrast essay. (You may want to consider the authors' attitudes toward issues such as crossing the border, immigrants who come to the United States illegally and what they do when they get to there, America's ability to absorb immigrants, and the government's ability to deal with illegal immigrants.) Develop outlines for an essay using both the point-by-point method and the block method. Give more weight to the contrasts.

Point-by-Point Method	Block Method

I. Point 1:
    A. Gilchrist's view
    B. Tierney's view
	I. Gilchrist's View of Illegal Immigration
	    A.
	    B.
	    C.

II. Point 2:
    A. Gilchrist's view
    B. Tierney's view
	II. Tierney's View of Illegal Immigration
	    A.
	    B.
	    C.

III. Point 3:
    A. Gilchrist's view
    B. Tierney's view	

C. ESSAY QUESTIONS

Write an essay on one of the topics. Use ideas, vocabulary, and writing techniques from this unit.

1. Write a comparison / contrast essay. Be sure to give more weight to either comparisons or contrasts. Choose one of the following topics to compare and contrast:

   a. Early immigrants vs. today's immigrants to your country

   b. American attitudes vs. the attitudes in your country toward immigrants

2. Do you believe that the U.S. government should try to protect the illegal immigrants who are already living in the United States, or should it try to deport them because they have violated the law? Be sure to include the opponent's view and your refutation.

3. What should be done to keep illegal immigrants from crossing borders? Do you agree with Gilchrist that governments should build stronger barriers, or do you see other solutions to the problem?

The Right to Die vs. The Right to Life

http://www.cartoonstock.com

I. ANTICIPATING THE ISSUE

Discuss your answers to the questions.

1. Look at the title. Look at the cartoon. What do you think the issue of this unit will be?

2. What is the message or humor of the cartoon?

3. What do you know about the right-to-die vs. the right-to-life controversy?

Read the text.

With unprecedented advances in medical technology, a debate has developed over whether a person on life support has the right to die. On one side of the debate are those who say that withdrawing a feeding tube or turning off a **respirator** gives doctors the power to take another person's life. On the other side is the view that fundamentally personal decisions about whether to continue living in an irreversible coma should be left to an individual or a family. This debate over **euthanasia**, the act of ending the life of an individual suffering from a terminal illness or incurable condition, involves conflicting **ethics**: moral, religious, and even political. As we move forward, these ethics will involve the lives, deaths, and destinies of more and more people.

One of the most widely reported cases in the euthanasia debate was the Nancy Cruzan case, which involved a 32-year-old woman from Missouri who existed for many years in a "persistent **vegetative** state" after a car accident. Her parents lived with the **trauma** of their daughter's **coma** for years before deciding to do something. Although she had rested in a **serene** state in her hospital bed for seven years, they did not want to continue treatment that would keep her in the state they knew Nancy would not want to be in. But when her parents **petitioned the court** to disconnect the feeding tube that was keeping Nancy alive, their request was ultimately denied. The lower-court ruling was later supported by the Supreme Court. Without "clear and convincing evidence" that Nancy Cruzan would have wanted her life-sustaining treatment to end, the Court held that the state is free to carry out its interest in "the protection and preservation of human life." Right-to-life activists have used the Court's decision to support their cause.

A less well-known case involved an 88-year-old woman from New York whose sister had obtained legal permission to remove her feeding tube, but that permission was later withdrawn. The woman's doctors had given the **prognosis** that she would remain in a hopeless state with no chance of recovery. However, before the feeding tube was removed, she improved and began talking and eating on her own. The doctors could not explain how the woman had **revived**, and they defined her improvement as a **miracle**. Later, when the woman was asked what she would wish to have done in her case, she responded, "These are difficult decisions," and went back to sleep. The next day she said that she wanted to wait to make a decision. Right-to-life activists have pointed to this case too to support their defense of what they call "vulnerable people."

Right-to-die activists, in contrast, contend that decisions about treatment for the dying should belong to the patients and their families. Other court cases have, in fact, ruled in their favor. When Paul Brophy, a firefighter, lapsed into a vegetative state, his wife managed to get hospital officials to remove his feeding tube, as he had stated that he would never want to live in a coma. Many people now write "living wills" stating their wish for euthanasia if they ever end up in a vegetative state. Patients who can make their wishes known are also being granted the right to end their lives. Larry McAfee, who was paralyzed from the neck down in a motorcycle accident, said that he did not want to live in his present state. A judge ruled that he could unhook his respirator and die, supporting McAfee's belief that it was not prolonging his life but prolonging his death. In still another case, Dr. Jack Kevorkian assisted an Alzheimer's[1] patient in dying with his "suicide machine," a machine he had created to help terminally ill patients end their lives. The machine caused the woman to die of a massive heart attack. The court did not find the doctor guilty of murder, as the patient had clearly chosen and administered her own death. Many people, in fact, found the patient to be a courageous pioneer, as she had taken control of the circumstances of her own death before it was too late.

The debate over euthanasia will only become more complex as medical technology continues to grow and improve. There are those who contend that euthanasia will soon become just a routine medical treatment, whereas others believe that its potential power for ending people's lives will prevent it from becoming a solution for human suffering. Most people hope neither they nor their family members will ever have to confront this issue.

A. VOCABULARY

Look at the boldfaced words and phrases in the Background Reading. Try to determine their meaning from the context. Complete each sentence to show that you understand the meaning of the boldfaced word. Compare your sentences with those of another student. Use a dictionary if necessary.

1. A **respirator** is used to help someone _____

   _____.

2. **Euthanasia** has not yet been accepted for humans, but it has been for

   _____.

3. One place that children might learn **ethics** is in _____

   _____.

4. If someone is in a **vegetative** state, he or she cannot _____

   _____.

5. If you experience a **trauma**, you probably feel _____

   _____.

6. A **coma** is often described as a deep _____

   _____.

---

[1]*Alzheimer's*: a serious disease that causes the deterioration of mental ability

7. If someone has a **serene** look on her face, she probably looks _____

_____ .

8. You might have to **petition the court** if you _____

_____ .

9. If a doctor's **prognosis** is not good for a terminally ill patient, it usually

means _____

_____ .

10. If a person becomes unconscious but is then **revived**, he or she can

_____ .

11. An example of a **miracle** is _____

_____ .

B. SUMMARIZING THE ISSUE

Work in small groups. Take notes on the following points from the Background Reading. Summarize the issue.

1. The issue (*state in your own words*): _____

_____

_____

2. Proponents' (of euthanasia) arguments: _____

_____

_____

3. Opponents' (of euthanasia) arguments: _____

_____

_____

C. VALUES CLARIFICATION

Work in small groups. Discuss your answers to the questions on the next page.

1. Do you tend to agree with the right-to-die or the right-to-life advocates? Who is best able to decide the future of a comatose or terminally ill person: family, lawyers, the courts, religious leaders, or someone else? Why?

2. Is the situation of a person who is not in a coma but who knows that he or she will soon die or deteriorate from a disease different from that of a comatose person? Should people who can make clear decisions about their destiny be allowed to choose death?

III. OPINION 1: LISTENING

A. LISTENING FOR THE MAIN IDEA

Listen to the commentary. Check the statement that best summarizes the commentator's main idea.

❑ 1. To allow someone to die takes courage.

❑ 2. The right to die cannot be accepted until we answer specific ethical questions.

❑ 3. Keeping people alive on life-support systems can be cruel.

B. LISTENING FOR DETAILS

Listen again and circle the best answer to each question. Compare your answers with those of another student. Listen again if necessary.

1. What is often argued?
   a. who should end a life
   b. when a life should be ended
   c. why a life was ended

2. What happened to Philip Gerard's mother?
   a. She was diagnosed with Parkinson's disease.
   b. She was admitted to the hospital.
   c. She lived through a heart attack.

3. What difficult choice did Gerard's father have to make?
   a. which treatment to use in his wife's illness
   b. whether to let his wife die
   c. whether to pressure the doctors to save her

4. The doctor's prognosis was that Gerard's mother would _____.
   a. probably come out of her coma
   b. suffer more brain damage
   c. always be in a vegetative state

5. Why wasn't the family allowed to let her die?
   a. Under state law, once she was on a respirator, she had to stay on it.
   b. A court order refused the family the right.
   c. She had a chance of living for 10 more years.

6. Gerard's mother's coma can be best described as _____.
   a. serene
   b. convulsive
   c. nervous

7. Why didn't Gerard turn off his mother's machine?
   a. He was afraid she wouldn't die in peace.
   b. Someone would have found out within a few hours.
   c. He wasn't courageous enough.

8. Why did the hospital wean his mother off the life-support system?
   a. She could only breathe through a tube in her throat.
   b. She had lost too much weight to continue full treatment.
   c. State law required a gradual reduction.

9. What conclusion does Gerard reach about this experience?
   a. Euthanasia is an ethical issue that needs far more debate.
   b. Human beings are basically cruel.
   c. The prolonging of his mother's life was inhumane.

C. TEXT COMPLETION AND DISCRETE LISTENING

Read the commentary. Fill in the missing words. Then listen again to check your answers. If your answers differ from the commentary, ask your teacher if they are acceptable alternatives.

Introduction

It is often argued that no one on _____ is equipped to judge the
                                          1

proper moment to end a life. But, in fact, people make those decisions every day.

And commentator Philip Gerard found sometimes they live to _____
                                                                     2

their choices.

Commentary

Just over a year ago, after fighting Parkinson's disease for almost ten years, my

mother suffered a _____ heart attack. She survived it only because she
                          3

was already in the hospital. She stopped breathing for at least eight minutes, possibly

as long as half an hour, before she was _____ by extraordinary means:
                                              4

defibrillator, adrenaline, the whole crash-cart, code-blue[2] scene. My father got a phone call demanding that he make an immediate choice: Put my mother on a _____ or let her die right then. Under pressure and unprepared for the awful circumstances, my father made the instinctive human choice: Try to save her.

    At the hospital, the doctors gave us their _____. For my mother to come out of her coma would be a _____ and a hideous one. The massive brain damage would leave her in a persistent _____ state. Then, the family decided, unhook the machines and let her die. Impossible, the doctors said. Under state law, once my mother was _____ up to the machine, she could not be unhooked without a court order. She might live for as long as a decade. My father would have to _____ the court to allow his wife of forty years to die.

    When I first heard the word coma, I imagined _____ catatonia[3]. But my mother's coma began as constant convulsions. With each _____ the respirator shoved into her lungs, her body shuddered. She frothed at the mouth. Her eyeballs rolled back, white, into her head. She was _____ down to the bed or she would have fallen to the floor. This lasted day and night for three days. After that, her nervous system virtually destroyed by the unrelieved _____ she quieted. My sisters and I took turns sleeping on a cot in my mother's room. We didn't want her to be _____ when she died.

    After a week of that, I recall lying awake into the small hours of a snowy morning, listening to the _____ of the monitors and the "suffing" of the respirator. I prayed for the _____ to turn off the machine and let her die in peace. It would have been easy—just click off the toggle. No one would have _____ for hours.

---

[2]*code blue:* a hospital emergency; in a hospital, a call for immediate medical assistance
[3]*catatonia:* total lack of movement; maintaining one position over a long period of time

I didn't have the courage.

My mother _____ three months. In the end, she was breathing
         19

through a tube permanently inserted in her throat. She _____ almost
         20

nothing. The doctors were keeping tissue alive, but the woman was long gone.

Honoring state law, the doctors _____ her off the respirator a little
         21

each day, forcing her to labor for every breath. They said she was in no pain, but

her face contorted and her body convulsed. Then she died.

You can argue the fine medical _____ of the thing. All I can add
         22

is this: I'd whip any man who treated a dog so cruelly.

IV.   OPINION 2: READING

A. READING FOR THE MAIN IDEA

Read the editorial. Check the statement that best summarizes the author's main idea.

❑ 1. It is costing society a great deal of money to keep people alive at any cost.

❑ 2. Living wills may be the best solution for unreasonable life support.

❑ 3. We must work toward respecting life, as we don't know the consequences
of euthanasia.

More on When to Die
by William F. Buckley, Jr. ....

I had at school a most **provocative** professor who liked mean questions, meanly formulated, because he liked to make his students think—"an agonizing alternative in your case," he might have said. One day it was announced that medical science had come through with a cure for, I forget what it was: some form of pneumonia. "What," the professor said, "are we supposed to die of?" And indeed if it were all an abstract game, and we counted 977 **extant** terminal diseases for each one of which medical science in due course came up with a cure, that would leave us nothing to die from save just plain decomposition of the flesh. It is generally agreed, if I read science correctly, that this is the one process that cannot be **arrested**. Inevitably, human beings being rational animals, thought is given to such questions as: Are there preferable ways to die than through biological decomposition?

A provocative book was published last year. It is called *Setting Limits*, with the explanatory subtitle, *Medical Goals in an Aging Society*. Its author, Daniel Callahan, is what one calls a bioethicist, someone who considers the ethical implications of biological developments. Mr. Callahan is the director of the Hastings Center, which he founded, and which inquires into such questions as—well, setting "limits" to **viable** lifetimes.

Callahan tells us that at the current rate of increase in **longevity**, the cost of maintaining the most senior population in America will by the end of the century[4] (which is not very far away) come to $200 billion a year. Mr. Callahan is not a pennypincher, but his point is that we may be engaged in **subsidizing** a great deal of agony as the result of our **preoccupation** with keeping people alive at any cost.

Most Americans are familiar with the creeping availability of what the lawyers call "living wills." These vary from state to state but have in common their search for a legal instrument by which an individual can, with **forethought**, specify the conditions under which he desires to be permitted to die. What Callahan uniquely advances is the idea of a living will in effect generally accepted by society at large, and one that focuses on a particular age. For instance, how would one greet the proposal that no publicly funded nursing home or hospital could finance a costly operation (say a heart bypass) for anyone over the age of 85?

The prospect of a corporate position on the right age to die is properly horrifying. Callahan goes so far as to include as an acceptable **stratagem**, the removal of food and water from old people who are **insensate** and would not feel the pain of their **mortal** deprivation. Such a proposal is shocking to moralist Nat Hentoff of *The Village Voice*, who comments, "If an old person is diagnosed as being in a **chronic** vegetative state (some physicians screw up[5] this diagnosis), the Callahan plan **mandates** that the feeding tube be denied or removed. No one is certain whether someone actually in a persistent vegetative state can feel what's going on while being starved to death. If there is sensation, there is no more horrible way to die." And then medical experts tell you that the cost of feeding insensate people is about the most inexpensive thing in medicine. True, it costs $20,000 a year to maintain someone in a nursing home. But to feed such a person through tubes costs only $10 per day.

The root question—here Hentoff wins the argument, I think—is moral, not **empirical**. If life is a divine gift, as Christians are taught to believe it is, then interruptions of it by acts of commission (suicide) or omission (a refusal to accept medical aid) are wrong. What the bioethicists search for is the ground in between. And the influence here of Pope Pius XII's exhortation in 1957 is critical for many Catholics and non-Catholics. What he said was that although no one may **collude** in any act of suicide, neither is the Christian required to take "extraordinary measures" to maintain life. In the famous case of Karen Ann Quinlan in New Jersey, the priest and the courts authorized the removal of the respirator from the comatose patient (ironically, she lived on for nine years).

The whole business **torments**, especially since more and more people have come into personal contact with the dying patient who comes to look upon medicine as a form of **torture**, given that its effect is to prolong life, and to prolong life for some is to prolong pain. No doubt, in the years to come, a working formula of sorts will emerge. It is critically important that it accept the moral implications of the question. If a society is ready for euthanasia, it has rejected the primary attribute of life: namely, that it is God-given. ∎

From the "On the Right" column by William F. Buckley, Jr. Copyright © 1988, Dist. Universal Press Syndicate. Reprinted with permission. All rights reserved.

---

[4]the twentieth century
[5]*screw up*: do incorrectly

B. READING FOR DETAILS

The following statements refer to ideas expressed in the article, but only some of them support the author's opinion. The others refer to what people who oppose his views have said. Decide which statements support Buckley's (*B*) opinions and which statements refer to the opposition's (*O*) opinions. Write *B* or *O* next to each statement. Compare your answers with those of another student. If your answers differ, go back to the text to find out why.

_____ 1. There may be preferable ways to die than through biological decomposition.

_____ 2. We may need to explore the idea of setting limits to viable lifetimes.

_____ 3. We are spending too much money to keep people alive.

_____ 4. A "living will" for society may be necessary in the future.

_____ 5. It is acceptable to remove food and water from old people who are insensate.

_____ 6. It is not expensive to feed a person through tubes.

_____ 7. Euthanasia is a moral, not an empirical, question.

_____ 8. Life is a divine gift.

_____ 9. No one should collude in any act of suicide.

_____10. To prolong life for some is to prolong pain.

_____11. Society must be ready for euthanasia.

C. WORD SEARCH

Write the boldfaced words from the editorial next to their definitions.

Nouns

1. _____: granting money for

2. _____: suffering

3. _____: state of mind in which something takes up all thoughts

4. _____: long life

5. _____: careful planning

6. _____: trick; device to deceive

Adjectives

7. _____: still in existence

8. _____: continual

9. _____: causing death

10. _____: able to exist

11. _____ relying on observation and experiment

12. _____: likely to cause interest or argument

13. _____: without the power to feel or experience

14. _____: stopped

Verbs

15. _____ causes severe suffering

16. _____ conspire; plot

17. _____ orders; requires

V. SYNTHESIZING TWO OPINION PIECES

A. DISTINGUISHING OPINIONS

Authors can have different viewpoints, but their opinions can sometimes be similar. Review the commentary and the editorial. Work in groups. Discuss whether Philip Gerard and / or Willam F. Buckley would agree with the statements below. Check the box of who you think would agree. Discuss how and why the two men's opinions are the same or different.

For example, Gerard would probably agree with the first statement. His family was not allowed to unhook the machine, which caused his mother even greater suffering. However, Buckley would probably not agree. He rejects euthanasia and feels that a refusal to accept medical aid is wrong. He would probably not agree with a family's having this power.

	GERARD: (OPINION 1)	BUCKLEY: (OPINION 2)
Families should have the ultimate power to decide the fate of a family member in a persistent vegetative state.	✓	
Extraordinary measures should be taken if it means keeping a person alive.		
Modern medicine can be torture.		
Euthanasia may be the least cruel treatment for a patient.		
We need to set limits to viable lifetimes, especially in an aging society.		
"Living wills" are a good solution to the problems posed by modern technology.		
It is costing society too much money to keep people alive at all costs.		

B. GIVING YOUR OPINION

Give your opinions on the statements in Part A. Discuss them with the other students in your group.

C. VOCABULARY REINFORCEMENT: Word Forms

Work in small groups. Fill in the missing word forms for each vocabulary item in the chart. (An *X* has been placed in the box if there is no related word form.) Use a dictionary if necessary.

NOUNS	VERBS	ADJECTIVES	ADVERBS
chronicity	X	chronic	
coma	X		X
ethics	X		
miracle	X		
preoccupation			X
		provocative	
		revived	X
	X	serene	
torture			
trauma			
		vegetative	vegetatively
	X	viable	viably

Read the sentences. Complete each sentence with the correct word form from the chart.

1. To decide whether euthanasia should be made legal is one of the most

   difficult _____ decisions of the decade.

2. Doctors can now _____ patients by extraordinary means when they suffer from heart attacks.

3. As we continue to develop technology that keeps people alive through artificial means, there is a greater chance that they will live as

_____ .

4. The _____ we observe in most comatose patients may be misleading, as we cannot know what they feel.

5. The concept that a group of individuals might decide what constitutes a(n)

_____ lifetime is alarming to many people.

6. Making life and death decisions is a(n) _____ experience for families of terminally ill patients.

7. Buckley _____ us to think about the appropriateness of mercy killing by stating that if a society is ready for euthanasia, it has rejected the primary attribute of life.

8. _____ ill patients spend much of their time in doctors' offices and hospitals.

9. The only way doctors could explain the 88-year-old woman's recovery after her feeding tube had been removed was that her revival was a

_____ .

10. Many people have come to believe that prolonging a terminally ill patient's

life is more _____ than generous.

11. Some people say that it is only in industrialized countries that people can

afford to have a _____ with the right to-die issue.

12. Some _____ patients have stayed alive in hospital beds for many years.

A. CASE STUDY: Death with Dignity in Oregon

The following reading presents a true case that raises the issue of whether doctor-assisted suicide should be legalized. Study the case.

Patients who once simply asked their doctors to help cure their diseases are now asking for more: aid in managing their deaths. In the state of Oregon, in the northwest United States, it is now legal for patients to make this request.

In the spring of 1998, a woman in her 80s who had been battling breast cancer for 20 years was the first person to legally end her life under the new "death with dignity" law in Oregon. She was having great difficulty breathing, and her doctor had told her that she had less than two months to live. However, her regular doctor would not prescribe the lethal dose of medicine she desired to end her life. Through a right-to-die group, she found a doctor willing to prescribe the drugs. Before her suicide, she said in a taped statement, "I'm looking forward to it. I will be relieved of all the stress I have." She died peacefully 25 minutes after taking the pills.

Voters in the state of Oregon twice approved a "death with dignity" law for their state. The law makes doctor-assisted suicide legal under certain conditions. When the law was upheld after several appeals, one 56-year-old Oregon woman with ovarian cancer stated, "It's important to have the option. Terminally ill people will find comfort from the fact that it's there." However, another terminally ill woman said legal doctor-assisted suicide was a "Pandora's box"—potentially leading to terrible acts, including mercy killings in which people who care for the terminally ill act on their own decisions about when euthanasia should occur. These two women's opinions echo the positions of the powerful political and religious organizations that have led the battles for and against doctor-assisted suicide in Oregon. The politician who sponsored the law, Barbara Coombs Lee, said that the law reflected the will of the people of Oregon. Leaders of some religious groups said the law was tragic and feared that Oregon would come to be known as the "death state."

Could this law make doctor-assisted suicide "routine" in Oregon? So far, it has not. To get assistance, patients must meet all the conditions outlined by the law. They must be terminally ill and have six months or less to live. They must make two verbal requests for assistance and convince two doctors that their request is sincere and voluntary. They must not be depressed. They must also be informed of "the feasible alternatives, including, but not limited to, comfort care, hospice care[6], and pain control." Finally, they must wait 15 days for their deadly dose of drugs. Lethal injection is not permitted under the law, so the drugs must be swallowed, which is not as easy for some patients and, in some rare cases, does not cause the desired quick death. However, many doctors find it difficult to inject patients directly with poison.

One major study reported that in 1998, the year after the death with dignity law overcame all legal challenges, 23 people sought assistance in dying under the law and 15 went through with it. Among the 23 who sought to commit suicide, the most common reason given was "concern about loss of autonomy or control of bodily functions." In the year 2007, 49 people legally committed suicide.

Although opposition from some religious, political, and even medical groups is strong, the idea of death with dignity is receiving attention across the United States. Lawmakers and

---

[6]*comfort care, hospice care*: treatments for terminally ill patients that aim to relieve suffering rather than cure illness

judges in the states of Colorado, Florida, Maine, Michigan, New York, and Washington, as well as the judges on the U.S. Supreme Court, have all wrestled with legal issues associated with the right to die. In 2005, the law was challenged by the George W. Bush administration but was upheld by the U.S. Supreme Court in *Gonzales v. Oregon*. It is still possible that the federal government will mount challenges to the Oregon law. The debate continues as more and more people take advantage of this law. Lawmakers and the public will eventually be forced to decide whether doctor-assisted suicide is murder or a service to humanity.

The Debate

Divide into two groups for a debate. The debate will focus on whether doctor-assisted suicide should be legalized. Use the information in the case to help you plan your arguments.

The Teams

1. **Team A: In favor of doctor-assisted suicide.** You believe that doctor-assisted suicide is a service to humanity. You are right-to-die advocates. You think doctors should be allowed to assist their patients in ending their lives.

2. **Team B: Opposed to doctor-assisted suicide.** You believe that doctor-assisted suicide is murder and that it has created a climate for pressured suicides. You are right-to-life advocates who cannot accept suicide as a means to end one's life. You think doctors should not be involved in their patients' desire to end their lives.

The Procedure

1. Select a moderator to lead the debate, and form teams.

2. Teams A and B prepare their arguments in small groups, citing evidence from the case and from the readings, and select a moderator.

3. Teams A and B face each other for a debate.

4. Team A begins with a one-minute presentation.

5. Team B responds in one minute or less.

6. The teams continue in this fashion. A member of a team is not allowed to speak until someone from the opposite team has made a counterargument.

7. After the debate, the moderator evaluates the strength of both arguments.

B. DISCUSSION QUESTIONS

Work in groups. Discuss your answers to the questions.

1. Go back to the questions in the values clarification exercise on pages 128–129. Do you have the same opinions now, or have you changed your opinions in any way after examining the views of others?

2. In your opinion, what role should doctors take in advising patients and / or their families in these cases? What is their responsibility?

3. According to the Hemlock Society, an organization that promotes public awareness and acceptance of euthanasia, more than 70 percent of people favor laws allowing doctors to assist terminally ill patients who wish to die. If laws are passed to allow this, what effect will it have on society?

VII. WRITING

A. GRAMMAR: Active and Passive Participial Phrases

Notice   Notice the highlighted verbs in these sentences from the commentary:

> **Honoring** state law, the doctors weaned her off the respirator a little each day, **forcing** her to labor for every breath.
> Under pressure and **unprepared** for the awful circumstances, my father made the instinctive human choice: Try to save her.

Which of the verbs is an active participle? Which is a passive participle? In what type of writing do we generally see these verb forms?

Explanation   Participles tend to occur more frequently in descriptive prose and less frequently in factual, scientific writing. They tend to evoke a visual image in the mind of the listener or reader.

Active Participles

In the first example, *honoring* and *forcing* are both active participles. They both describe what the doctors are doing.

The present participial phrase contains the present participle of the verb.

In the active voice, the present participial phrase indicates that the action in the phrase and the action in the main clause take place at the same time. In the quote, the *honoring* and the *forcing* both occurred at the same time as the verb in the main clause, *weaned*.

When the action in the participial phrase happens before the action in the main clause, whether the main clause is past or present, the perfect participial phrase (*having* + past participle) is used.

For example:

Having weaned her off the respirator, the doctors allowed her to die.

Passive Participles

In the second example, *unprepared* is a passive participle. It gives a reason for the result expressed in the main clause.

The passive participial phrase contains the past participle of the verb.

Unlike in active participial phrases, the time relationship in these phrases is not always significant. This is because the passive participle usually functions as an adjective and is descriptive in nature.

The perfect progressive participle (*having* + *been* + past participle) may also be used in descriptive cases in the passive voice.

For example:

Having been pressured by doctors, my father made the instinctive human choice.

Exercise

Fill in the blanks with the active or passive participle of the verb in parentheses. Choose the correct form of each verb. Each sentence refers to Philip Gerard's commentary.

1. _____ Parkinson's disease for almost 10 years, his mother
   (fight)
   suffered a massive heart attack.

2. _____ in the hospital, she could be revived by
   (be)
   extraordinary means.

3. The doctor called his father, _____ that he make a choice.
   (demand)

4. _____ and _____, his father made the
   (confuse)   **(shock)**
   instinctive human choice to save her.

5. _____ the prognosis, the family decided to unhook
   (give)
   the machines.

6. _____ state law, the hospital told the family that they could
   (respect)
   not unhook the machine without a court order.

7. _____ the word "coma" the first time, Gerard pictured a
   (hear)

   state of serenity.

8. Her nervous system, _____ by unrelieved trauma, finally
   (destroy)

   broke down.

9. _____ awake into the small hours of a snowy morning,
   (lie)

   Gerard listened to the hum of the monitors and the "suffing" of the

   respirator.

10. _____ for courage, Gerard thought of turning off the
    (hope)

    machine.

11. She had to breathe independently, _____ off the respirator.
    (wean)

B. WRITING STYLE: Concession

Notice Read the following sentences from William F. Buckley's editorial. Why does he make these comments in his argument against euthanasia?

> *True, it costs $20,000 a year to maintain someone in a nursing home.*

> *The whole business torments, especially since more and more people have come into personal contact with the dying patient who comes to look upon medicine as a form of torture, given that its effect is to prolong life, and to prolong life for some is to prolong pain.*

Explanation Effective writers of opinion essays often use concession in their argument. If writers acknowledge the truth of opposing arguments, their own argument can be strengthened. By conceding facts and opinions of the opposition, writers show that they have thought through an issue, examining the arguments from a wider perspective.

Buckley makes two concessions in his argument. By acknowledging the fact that it is expensive to maintain someone in a nursing home, he shows that he is aware of the financial issues. But then he reinforces his own argument by pointing out that feeding a person through tubes only costs $10 per day. By acknowledging the fact that prolonging life can sometimes prolong pain, he shows that he has considered the difficulties that patients and their families sometimes go through. But then he reinforces his own argument by bringing up the moral implications of not providing medicine to dying patients.

Concession sentences are generally integrated into paragraphs, but sometimes they appear as full paragraphs in an essay. They should never be given more weight than the sentences and paragraphs supporting the writer's thesis, however.

Concession statements can be introduced in two ways and are usually followed by the writer's argument.

Adverbial conjunctions: In adverbial conjunctions, the concession is in the dependent clause and the main clause gives the writer's point of view:

Although
Even though
While
In spite of the fact that
Despite the fact that

For example:

***Even though** prolonging life for some is to prolong pain, it is critically important that we accept the moral implications of euthanasia.*

Transitions: Here the concession is an independent clause. This is followed by a contrasting independent clause that gives the writer's point of view:

True
Admittedly
Without doubt
Clearly
Undoubtedly

For example:

*"**True**, it costs $20,000 a year to maintain someone in a nursing home. But to feed such a person through tubes costs only $10 per day."*

Exercise

Read the following points made to support Buckley's opinion. How might advocates of euthanasia argue with his views? (You may want to consider the views of Gerard.) Use Buckley's ideas to create concession statements and then present a contrasting argument. Use the concession language given in parentheses to write your statements:

1. The cost of feeding a comatose patient is only $10 per day. (Admittedly . . .)

   _____

2. Living wills may encourage the setting of "limits" to viable lifetimes. (Although . . .)

   _____

3. The prospect of a corporate position on the right age to die is horrifying. (Clearly . . .)

   _____

4. Some physicians screw up a patient's diagnosis as being in chronic vegetative state. (Even though . . .)

_____

5. No one knows whether someone in a persistent vegetative state can feel what's going on while a feeding tube is being removed. (In spite of the fact that . . .)

_____

6. Life is a divine gift and interruptions of it by acts of commission or omission are wrong. (Undoubtedly . . .)

_____

7. Euthanasia is a rejection of the primary attribute of life. (While . . .)

_____

C. ESSAY QUESTIONS

Write an essay on one of the numbered topics. Use ideas, vocabulary, and writing techniques from this unit. For question 1, try to incorporate the following:

- an introductory paragraph that presents both sides of the argument and clearly states your thesis

- paragraphs (at least three) that develop your argument with supporting evidence

- a conclusion that reinforces the position you have taken and ends with a new idea (a warning, prediction, value judgment) that has not been mentioned before

1. Do you believe life-support systems, respirators, and feeding tubes are devices that sustain life or prolong dying? Write an essay in which you express your opinion.

2. Write about a time when you had to make a decision that was a matter of life and death. Develop a thesis through your narration.

The Global Village

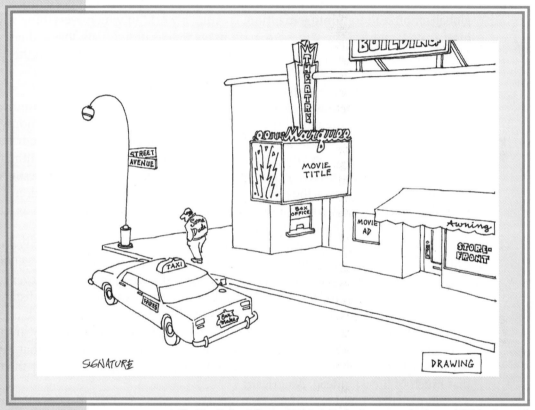

I. ANTICIPATING THE ISSUE

Discuss your answers to the questions.

1. Look at the title. Look at the cartoon. What do you think the issue of this unit will be?

2. What is the message or humor of the cartoon?

3. In your opinion, what are the benefits of globalization? What are the drawbacks?

Read the text.

With modern information and communication technologies making the world smaller, many people question whether globalization is more positive or more negative. As nations become more integrated into a single global market, our traditional cultural barriers are being **breached** and more opportunities for international exchange are being created. But with the fading borders between nations, new questions arise. Does economic growth from the global market tend to favor the rich and leave the poor behind? And, perhaps most importantly, will globalization lead to **homogenization**, creating a world in which everything will look, sound, and feel the same? Are nations, as well as individuals, losing their identities as they become more globalized? Some have **prophesied** that in the not-too-distant future, American tastes, habits, and values will completely dominate the world. Is globalization really the same as "Americanization"?

One of the strongest arguments against globalization is that poorer countries will not benefit from the global market. Inequalities will widen, and the poor will be left out as the rich become more prosperous. Developed countries already have a greater share of resources, and globalization will only reinforce their wealth and power. The richest countries, including the United States, will pool their resources and gain a monopoly over the global market. Some believe that globalization should proceed, if at all, under a set of restrictive new rules on issues such as labor, the environment, and human rights.

Will everyone's worldview soon be **seen through a prism** of America? People drink Coke and Pepsi around the world. McDonald's now has more than 25,000 outlets in 119 countries; a new restaurant opens somewhere in the world every 17 hours. People around the world watch the same American movies and listen to the same American music. In recent decades, we have witnessed the growth of American mega-malls all over the world. The Internet functions primarily in the English language and is dominated by American content. It is estimated that 70 percent of Internet Web sites are American. Have people begun to **register** the fact that much of life is, indeed, American?

But globalization does not necessarily have to mean Americanization. Rather, it could be a blending of many different cultures. For example, there is currently a **mass migration** of people from other nations to the United States, one that is unprecedented. Immigrants and refugees import their cultural values into the United States as much as they assimilate American culture. Many **would-be refugees** manage to make their way to the United States and import their cultural values as well. In fact, America is not really a **melting pot** in the sense that immigrants' cultures dissolve into American culture. In fact, they remain distinct. Just as American tastes and values have influenced the world, American tastes and values have been influenced: They have become more **eclectic**—in food, music, and even religion.

Finally, one thing people fear most about globalization is a loss of individual identity. They fear that a sense of **shallowness** might come from living in "the global village," as tastes and cultural attitudes become more homogeneous. Human beings enjoy being different, feeling unique. Perhaps this is why one reaction to our global world seems to be an increased attachment to traditional ethnic customs. In many cities around the world, **ethnic enclaves**, rather than integrated communities, have formed and lasted.

Yet with globalization comes a form of **cosmopolitanism**. People's perspective is more worldwide today, less narrow. New relationships have been **forged** over the Internet. Students in China now correspond with students in Canada in chat rooms on the Internet. Professionals from all branches of life can share their research questions and answers internationally. It could be said that people are forming new identities as they interact with a greater number of people worldwide.

Globalization appears to be inevitable: We cannot go back. Driven primarily by information technology and capital markets, its force is transforming the world with extraordinary speed. Many believe that coping with this transformation is our greatest challenge.

A. VOCABULARY

Match the boldfaced words and phrases in the Background Reading with their definitions below. Write the word or phrase next to its definition.

1. _____: familiarity with many people and places

2. _____: formed, created

3. _____: lack of depth; superficiality

4. _____: viewed from a particular perspective

5. _____: predicted

6. _____: culturally distinct units within a territory

7. _____: broken

8. _____: people who would like to leave their country because of danger, war, or persecution

9. _____: process of blending

10. _____: large movements of people from one place to another

11. _____: become clear about; make sense of

12. _____: situation or place in which many cultures blend to form a new one

13. _____: made up of or combining elements from a variety of sources

B. SUMMARIZING THE ISSUE

Work in small groups. Take notes on the negative and positive effects of globalization. Summarize the issue.

Negative Effects of Globalization	Positive Effects of Globalization
_____	_____
_____	_____
_____	_____

C. VALUES CLARIFICATION

Work in small groups. Discuss your answer to the question.

Look at your notes in Part B. Do you think globalization is more positive or more negative?

III.   OPINION 1: LISTENING

A. LISTENING FOR THE MAIN IDEA

Listen to the commentary and circle the best answer to each question.

1. Who implies that globalization is the same as Americanization?
   a. the commentator
   b. the commentator's friend
   c. Madonna

2. What has broken down cultural barriers?
   a. war
   b. more travel
   c. technology

3. How does the commentator see the process of globalization?
   a. as cosmopolitanism
   b. as shallowness
   c. as integration

4. According to the commentator, what happens to our identity as our world changes?
   a. It becomes more fixed.
   b. It gets reconstructed.
   c. It becomes more confused.

B. LISTENING FOR DETAILS

Listen again. Write *T* (true) or *F* (false) for each statement. Compare your answers with those of another student. Listen again if necessary.

_____ 1. We can stop immigration, but we cannot stop the flow of cultures around the world.

_____ 2. The commentator's friend thinks too many people are eating at McDonald's.

_____ 3. Thai food is usually served with a French-style wine.

_____ 4. Globalization sometimes means Americanization to Americans.

_____ 5. The commentator's friend is an exception.

_____ 6. A teenager in Idaho now talks with her friend in Osaka on the Internet.

_____ 7. The commentator and his friend agree on the modern condition.

_____ 8. The concept of a melting pot in America has been challenged by ethnic enclaves.

_____ 9. Americans' tastes have become more southern and more Asian.

_____ 10. The number of people practicing Buddhism is growing in America.

_____ 11. Geography continues to form and fix American identity.

C. TEXT COMPLETION AND DISCRETE LISTENING

Read the commentary. Fill in the missing words. Then listen again to check your answers. If your answers differ from the commentary, ask your teacher if they are acceptable alternatives.

Introduction

A country may be able to pass laws to keep out would-be _____ or
                                                            1

other immigrants, but commentator Andrew Lam says it's much harder to

_____ the flow of cultures around the world.
        2

Commentary

A friend, well-traveled and educated, recently predicted the _____
                                                                    3

of globalization in very simple terms. "Everyone will be eating at McDonald's,

listening to Madonna, and shopping at mega-malls," he _____. That
                                                              4

we were sitting in a Thai restaurant in San Francisco eating stir-fry squid based in a pungent shrimp paste and drinking a very buoyant Cabernet did not occur to him as _____ . Nor did it seem to _____ that he
5   6
himself is the answer to his own fear of global _____ and
7
_____ . He speaks three languages fluently, listens to Stan Getz and
8
Cesaria Evora, and wouldn't be caught dead eating at any mega

_____ . I told him that globalization is not the same as
9
Americanization, though sometimes it's hard for Americans to make that

distinction. Furthermore, though _____ , my friend should no
10
longer perceive himself as an _____ .
11

    There's a _____ revolution taking place _____
12   13
our very noses. The Chinese businessman in Silicon Valley is constantly in touch

with his Shanghainese mother on _____ phone, and a blond
14
teenager in Idaho is making friends with a Japanese girl in Osaka in a

_____ room. Their friendship and community are easily
15

_____ , as if time and space and cultural barriers have been
16

_____ by their lilting modems and the blinking satellites above.
17
Ours is a world of fading borders and unprecedented mass _____
18
and of instantaneous information flow. People are _____ across
19
time zones and continents, taking references from two or three different cultures.

    Contrary to my friend, I see _____ , not shallowness, as our modern
20
condition. Indeed, Americans may see the world through our own

_____ , but America itself has radically changed. Little Saigon in
21
Orange County and the Cuban community in Miami are not places created out of

nostalgia but are vibrant and thriving ethnic _____ , a direct
22
challenge to the old idea of _____ pot and integration.
23

Americans' tastes, too, have gone _____ and far east these days.
                                              24

We want more chili in our sauce, practice tai chi, and fall in love with Ricky

Martin. All the while, Islam and _____ are two of the fastest-
                                        25

growing religions in America. Geography is no longer destiny. It is losing its grip

on human life everywhere and is quickly replaced by the realm of imagination. We

live now in a world where _____ is no longer fixed in stone but
                                    26

must be constructed and _____ .
                                27

To live in the global village, we need to view ourselves through many-color

_____ . In the process, we see all the dimensions of our quickly
        28

shifting world.

A. READING FOR THE MAIN IDEA

Read the article. Check the statement that best summarizes the author's main idea.

❑ 1. Globalization has caused more refugees than ever to leave their homelands.

❑ 2. We are all plugged into the same global circuit.

❑ 3. With globalization, our cultures are becoming more fragmented.

Are We Coming Apart or Together?
by Pico Iyer ·

If you like things that are new and different, our globalizing world is a dream. Plenty of folks, though, want things to stay the same.

It is a truth all but universally acknowledged that the more internationalism there is in the world, the more nationalism there will be: the more multinational companies, multicultural beings, and planetary networks are crossing and transcending borders, the more other forces will, as if in response, fashion new divisions and aggravate old ones. Human nature **abhors** a vacuum, and it is only natural, when people find themselves in a desert, without boundaries, that they will try to **assuage** their vulnerability by settling into a community. Thus fewer and fewer wars take place these days across borders, and more and more take place within them.

Many Americans, rejoicing in an unprecedented period of economic success and celebrating the new horizons opened up by our latest technologies, are likely to embrace the future as a dashing (if unknown) stranger who's appeared at our door to **whisk** us into a strange new world. Those who travel, though, are

(continued)

more likely to see rising **tribalism**, widening divisions and all the fissures that propel ever more of the world into what looks like anarchy. Fully 97 percent of the population growth that will bring our numbers up to 9 billion by the year 2050 will take place in developing countries, where conditions are scarcely better than they were a hundred years ago. In many cases, in fact, history seems to be moving backward (in modern Zimbabwe, to take but one example, the average life expectancy has **dwindled** from 70 to 38 in recent years because of AIDS). To travel today is to see a planet that looks more and more like a too typical downtown on a global scale: a small **huddle** of shiny high-rises reaching toward a multinational heaven, surrounded on every side by a wasteland of the poor, living in a state of almost biblical desperation. When people speak of a "**digital divide**," they are, in effect, putting into twenty-first-century technological terms what is an age-old cultural problem: that all the globalism in the world does not erase (and may in fact intensify) the differences between us. Corporate bodies stress connectedness, borderless economies, all the wired communities that make up our worldwide webs; those in Chechnya, Kosovo, or Rwanda remind us of much older forces. And even as America exports its dotcom optimism around the world, many other countries export their **primal animosities** to America.

Get in a cab near the Capitol, say, or the World Trade Center and ask the wrong question, and you are likely to hear a **tirade** against the Amhara or the Tigreans, Indians, or Pakistanis. If all the world's a global village, that means that the ancestral divisions of every place can play out in every other. And the very use of that comforting word "village" tends to distract us from the fact that much of the world is coming to resemble a global city (with all the gang warfare, fragmentation and generalized **estrangement** that those centers of affluence promote). When the past century began, 13 percent of humans lived in cities; by the time it ended, roughly 50 percent did.

The hope, in the face of these counterclockwise movements, is that we can be bound by what unites us, which we have ever more occasion to see; that the stirring visions of Thomas Paine or Martin Luther King Jr. have more **resonance** than ever, now that an American can meet a Chinese counterpart—in Shanghai or San Francisco (or many places in between)—and see how much they have in common. What Emerson called the Oversoul reminds us that we are joined not only by our habits and our urges and our fears but also by our dreams and that best part of us that intuits an identity larger than you or I. Look up, wherever you are, and you can see what we have in common; look down—or inside—and you can see something universal. It is only when you look around that you note divisions.

The fresher and more particular hope of the moment is that as more and more of us cross borders, we can step out of, and beyond, the old categories. Every time a Palestinian man, say, marries a Singhalese woman (and such unions are growing more common by the day) and produces a half-Palestinian, half-Singhalese child (living in Paris or London, no doubt), an Israeli or a Tamil is deprived of a tribal enemy. Even the Palestinian or Singhalese grandparents may be eased out of longtime prejudices. **Mongrelism**—the human equivalent of World Music and "**fusion culture**"—is the brightest child of fragmentation.

Yet the danger we face is that of celebrating too soon a global unity that only covers much deeper divisions. Much of the world is linked, more than ever before, by common surfaces: people on every continent may be watching Michael Jordan advertising Nike shoes on CNN. But beneath the surface, inevitably, traditional differences remain. George Bernard Shaw declared generations ago that England and America were two countries divided by a common language. Now the world often resembles 200 countries divided by a common frame of cultural reference. The number of countries on the planet, in the twentieth century, has more than tripled.

Beyond that, multinationals and machines tell us that we're all plugged into the same global circuit, without considering very much what takes place off-screen. China and India, to cite the two giants that comprise one in every three of the world's people, have recently begun to embrace the opportunities of the global marketplace and the conveniences of e-reality (and, of course, it is often engineers of Chinese and Indian origin who have made these new wonders possible). Yet for all that connectedness on an individual level, the Chinese government remains as reluctant as ever to play by the rules of the rest of the world, and Indian leaders make nuclear gestures as if Dr. Strangelove had just landed in Delhi. And as some of us are able to fly across continents for business or pleasure, others are propelled out of their homelands by poverty and necessity and war, in record numbers: the number of refugees in the world has gone up 1,000 percent since 1970.

It seems a safe bet, as we move toward the year 2025, that governments will become no more idealistic than they have ever been—they will always represent a community of interests. And corporations cannot afford to stress conscience or sacrifice before profit. It therefore falls to the individual, on her own initiative, to look beyond the divisions of her parents' time and find a common ground with strangers to apply the all-purpose adjective "global" to "identity" and "loyalty."

Never before in history have so many people, whether in Manhattan or in Tuva, been surrounded by so much that is alien (in customs, languages and neighborhoods). How we orient ourselves in the midst of all this foreignness and in the absence of the old certainties will determine how much our nations are disunited and how much we are bound by what Augustine called "things loved in common." ■

From *Time*, May 22, 2000.
© 2000 Time Inc. Reprinted by permission.

B. READING FOR DETAILS

Circle the letter that best completes each sentence, according to the author's opinion. Compare your answers with those of another student. Read the article again if necessary.

1. The more internationalism there is in the world _____.
   a. the less nationalism will develop
   b. the more companies will grow
   c. the more divisions will come back

2. When people find themselves alone, _____.
   a. they will look for the desert
   b. they will look for a community
   c. they will engage in more wars

3. Life expectancy in modern Zimbabwe is now _____.
   a. 97
   b. 70
   c. 38

4. The "digital divide" refers to _____.
   a. separation
   b. borderless economies
   c. dotcom optimism

5. In today's global city, one finds _____.
   a. the comfort of a village
   b. more gangs
   c. fewer people

6. Even with the negative effects of globalization, we can hope that

   _____.
   a. we can be bound by what we have in common
   b. we can travel to more places
   c. we can get rid of our urges and fears

7. We notice our divisions when we look _____.
    a. up
    b. inside
    c. around

8. One positive outcome of our borders merging is that _____.
    a. a Palestinian marries a Singhalese
    b. more people move from Paris to London
    c. people marry across race and culture

9. The danger in celebrating global unity is that _____.
    a. we create deeper divisions
    b. we do not notice traditional differences
    c. we further divide ourselves by language

10. The responsibility for finding a "global identity" lies with _____.
    a. the government
    b. corporations
    c. the individual

C. WORD SEARCH

Look at the boldfaced words in the editorial. Try to determine their meaning from the context. Complete each sentence to show that you understand the meanings of the boldfaced words. Compare your sentences with those of another student. Use a dictionary if necessary.

1. If you **abhor** your job, you will probably try to _____.

2. A mother will try to **assuage** her child's pain by _____.

3. Politicians are sometimes **whisked** away from reporters by their advisers because _____.

4. _____ is a larger concept of **tribalism**.

5. One reason the population has **dwindled** in some countries is because _____.

6. Friends might form a **huddle** when they _____.

7. The **digital divide** refers to the ever sharper division between wealthy and poor countries because of the increase in _____.

8. When **primal animosities** between nations are played out openly, the result is often _____.

9. The mother goes into a **tirade** at her teenage son whenever he

   _____.

10. Perhaps an immigrant feels the most **estrangement** in his or her new

    land when _____.

11. Martin Luther King Jr. was said to have great **resonance** with a crowd of

    people who listened to him because _____.

12. One effect of globalization could be **mongrelism**, or a mixing of cultures;

    an opposite effect could be _____.

13. _____ is an example of music born of **fusion culture**.

V. SYNTHESIZING TWO OPINION PIECES

A. DISTINGUISHING OPINIONS

There are several common themes in the two opinion pieces. Take notes on comments that relate to these themes. Compare your notes with those of another student.

THEMES	LAM: (OPINION 1)	IYER: (OPINION 2)
shallowness		
Americanization		
borders and divisions		
identity		
global village		
forming of community		
technology		
cultural reference		

B. GIVING YOUR OPINION

What is your opinion of globalization? For each theme in Part A, discuss with a partner whether you share the views of commentator Andrew Lam or writer Pico Iyer.

C. VOCABULARY REINFORCEMENT: Vocabulary / Concept Grid

Work in groups. Discuss the relationship of the vocabulary to the concepts.

Put a plus (+) in the box if there is a positive relationship between them (one causes the other, one is an example of the other, one supports the other).

Put a minus (–) in the box if there is a negative relationship between them (one contradicts the other, one is not an example of the other, one does not support the other).

Put a question mark (?) in the box if your group is unsure of the relationship or cannot agree. The first one has been done for you as a suggested answer.

Breached cultural barriers . . .
- *are negatively related (–) to nationalism because when cultural barriers are broken, people tend to become more international.*
- *are unclearly related (?) to tribalism because some might say that it would increase as a result of cultures coming together, whereas others might say that it would be diffused.*
- *are positively related (+) to globalization because, with globalization, cultures blend and differences are less apparent.*

	NATIONALISM	TRIBALISM	GLOBALIZATION
breached cultural barriers	–	?	+
cosmopolitanism			
dwindling life expectancy			
estrangement			
ethnic enclaves			
fading borders			
fusion culture			
global village			
homogenization			

	NATIONALISM	TRIBALISM	GLOBALIZATION
primal animosities			
shallowness			
unprecedented mass migration			
widening divisions and fissures			

VI. SPEAKING

A. CASE STUDY: José Bové's Attack against McDonald's

The following reading presents a true case that raises the issue of whether globalization is a positive or negative force in the world today.

Work in groups of three. Study the case. Put yourself in the role of one of the three judges who must decide whether José Bové should be sentenced to go to jail and pay a fine. Consider the prosecutor's recommendation to give a lighter sentence. Discuss the implications of this case and come to a verdict. Present your verdict to the rest of the class.

One day, without warning, José Bové, a French sheep farmer, along with nine companions, took a power saw and crowbars to a McDonald's restaurant that was under construction in his small hometown of Millau. Why would a French farmer who was educated in the United States want to dismantle the famous hamburger restaurant?

The attack was a symbolic one in that it represented an increasing rejection of *la malbouffe*—nasty food from abroad, as symbolized by McDonald's hamburgers. It was a direct response to the U.S. decision to raise tariffs 100 percent on Roquefort cheese, foie gras, and mustard. (Bové's sheep produce milk that helps make Roquefort.) This raising of tariffs had apparently been a retaliation for an earlier European ban on U.S. beef that contained hormones. Symbolically, the attack was against the excesses of globalization, or the multinational crusade to homogenize the world. "McDonald's represents globalization, multinationals, the power of the market," Bové said in an interview. "Then it stands for industrially produced food: bad for traditional farmers and bad for your health. And lastly, it's a symbol of America. It comes from the place where they not only promote globalization and industrially produced food but also unfairly penalize our peasants." Bové heads a farmers group in his region, the Confédération Paysanne, which is fighting these practices.

Bové was arrested and sent to prison for 20 days, which he was pleased about. "The judge did us a great service by throwing me in jail," Bové said. "We couldn't have asked for better publicity." A fund launched by the producers of Roquefort cheese received donations from all over the country that enabled him to be released on $17,000 bail. When he got out of prison, the militant was given many TV and newspaper interviews and quickly became a national hero.

(continued)

In fact, Bové has been embraced by the French president and taken to lunch by the French prime minister. Both have expressed sympathy for Bové's actions.

A group of American farmers even contributed $5,000 toward paying his bail after the McDonald's incident. According to one poll, 80 percent of the French public sympathized with Bové's attack on McDonald's.

Bové has become a popular symbol of the fear and animosity that many Europeans feel toward American-dominated globalization. They feel that globalization threatens their cultures and national identities. Bové strongly opposes the World Trade Organization (WTO), multinationals, and governments that push scientifically engineered food. He opposes the WTO, which, he says, dictates its own law on the opening of trade barriers. He has become one of the leaders of the world resistance against global capitalism and internationalized commerce and a hero in France as well as, paradoxically, the United States.

As a show of solidarity, at least 40,000 supporters and activists from around the world gathered in Millau. A public prosecutor has recommended that Bové receive a 10-month suspended sentence and that the nine other defendants receive suspended sentences of no longer than three months.

Meanwhile, another attack was made on a McDonald's in Quévert, in which a woman employee was killed. Although Bové was not involved in this incident, people have said that he, having started the antiglobalization movement, should be held responsible for similar events.

B. DISCUSSION QUESTIONS

Work in groups. Discuss your answers to the questions.

1. In his commentary, Andrew Lam makes the statement, "People are negotiating across time zones and continents, taking references from two or three different cultures." What does he mean by taking references from more than one culture? Can you think of any examples in your own life in which you take references from more than one culture?

2. In his article, Pico Iyer states, "Look up, wherever you are, and you can see what we have in common; look down—or inside—and you can see something universal. It is only when you look around that you note divisions." What do you think he means? Give examples to support his statement. Do you agree with him?

A. GRAMMAR: The Double Comparative

Notice Notice the structure *the more . . . , the more . . .* in the opening sentence of the second paragraph of the article. What is the relationship between the parts linked by *the more . . . , the more*?

> *It is a truth all but universally acknowledged that the more internationalism there is in the world, the more nationalism there will be.*

Explanation Structures with *the more / the less* + noun + *the more / the less* + noun are called double comparatives. There are two parts to this type of sentence; the second part shows the result of the first.

> *The more internationalism there is, the more nationalism there will be.*

= When there is more internationalism, there is more nationalism.

> *The more globalization we experience, the less integration we feel.*

= When we experience more globalization, we also feel less integration.

Notice that with double comparative nouns, the verb phrase is often dropped to produce a comparison of noun phrases.
    For this structure, the article *the* is used before each noun:

> *The more the globalization, the less the integration.*

Exercise 1

Complete the sentences with your own opinion. Use the double comparative structure.

1. The more technology advances, _____

   _____ .

2. The more users on the Internet, _____

   _____ .

3. The more time zones and borders are crossed, _____

   _____ .

4. The more the cosmopolitanism, _____

   _____ .

5. The less geography determines our destiny, _____

_____ .

6. The less our world fixes our identity in stone, _____

_____ .

Exercise 2

Consider the ideas expressed in Pico Iyer's article. Rewrite the following sentences using the double comparative pattern *the more / the less . . . the more / the less.*

1. There is a rise of tribalism; consequently, there is an increase in anarchy.

_____

_____

2. America continues to export its dotcom optimism around the world. Other countries are expressing their animosities to America.

_____

_____

3. As more and more of us step across borders, we feel less confined by old categories.

_____

_____

4. We feel a global unity with common references such as Michael Jordan. The world continues to divide itself into fragmented countries.

_____

_____

B. WRITING STYLE: Illustration

Notice   Reread the first paragraph of Andrew Lam's commentary. How does the commentator's friend support his view that globalization is leading to Americanization? What examples does he give? How does the commentator support his view that globalization reflects internationalization rather than Americanization? What examples does he give?

Explanation Lam's friend uses examples to support his view. He cites the popularity of eating at McDonald's, listening to Madonna, and shopping at mega-malls as examples of this. The use of such examples makes ideas more concrete and lends support to generalizations.

There are generally two ways to support a main idea through illustration:

A series of examples (from Lam's commentary):

> *A friend, well-traveled and educated, recently predicted the evils of globalization in very simple terms. "Everyone will be **eating at McDonald's, listening to Madonna, and shopping at mega-malls**," he prophesied.*

One extended example (from Iyer's article):

> *Many Americans, rejoicing in an unprecedented period of economic success and celebrating the new horizons opened up by our latest technologies, are likely to embrace the future as a dashing (if unknown) stranger who's appeared at our door to whisk us into a strange new world. **Those who travel, though, are more likely to see rising tribalism, widening divisions and all the fissures that propel ever more of the world into what looks like anarchy. Fully 97 percent of the population growth that will bring our numbers up to 9 billion by the year 2050 will take place in developing countries, where conditions are scarcely better than they were a hundred years ago. In many cases, in fact, history seems to be moving backward (in modern Zimbabwe, to take but one example, the average life expectancy has dwindled from 70 to 38 in recent years because of AIDS). To travel today is to see a planet that looks more and more like a too typical downtown on a global scale: a small huddle of shiny high-rises reaching toward a multinational heaven, surrounded on every side by a wasteland of the poor, living in a state of almost biblical desperation.***

Exercise 1

Review Andrew Lam's commentary. Focus on the examples he uses throughout his commentary. Write the series of examples he gives to support his opinion on the following:

1. Transnational revolution: _____

_____

2. Challenge to melting pot and integration: _____

_____

3. Americans' eclectic tastes: _____

_____

Exercise 2

Each of the following is a topic sentence that could be developed into an interesting paragraph with examples. Choose one or two and write a complete paragraph for each. Develop the main idea with either a series of examples or one extended example.

1. The more global we are, the more cosmopolitan we become.

2. The United States is no longer a melting pot.

3. Identity is no longer fixed in stone.

4. The "digital divide" only emphasizes the differences between us.

5. The "global village" is really a "global city."

C. ESSAY QUESTIONS

Write an essay on one of the numbered topics. Use ideas, vocabulary, and writing techniques from this unit. Try to incorporate the following:

- an introductory paragraph that presents the various sides of the argument and clearly states your thesis

- paragraphs (at least three) that develop your argument with supporting evidence

- a conclusion that reinforces the position you have taken and ends with a new idea (a warning, prediction, value judgment) that has not been mentioned before

1. What are the advantages and disadvantages of globalization? Write an essay in which you discuss both the positive and negative consequences of this process. Use personal examples as well as any examples from the commentary or article with which you agree. In your conclusion, state whether you think the advantages or disadvantages are greater.

2. Do you agree that globalization is the same as Americanization? Why or why not? Discuss at least three examples that support your opinion.

For Every Winner, There's a Loser

Lottery

I. ANTICIPATING THE ISSUE

Discuss your answers to the questions.

1. Look at the title. Look at the cartoon. What do you think the issue of this unit will be?

2. What is the message or humor of the cartoon?

3. What do you know about legalized gambling?

Read the text.

Until 1964 most forms of gambling were illegal in the United States. Since then, however, more and more states have legalized gambling in order to raise **revenue**. The U.S. gambling industry has gone from an attitude of "prohibition" to one of "promotion," as all but two states now have legalized gambling as a solution to their depressed economies.

Most states in the United States now depend on revenues from state lotteries and use them for good causes, such as improving public education, maintaining state parks, and developing environmental programs. For example, the Arizona lotto contributed more than $78 million to senior citizen programs and transportation. In Oregon, there is a current proposal to use lottery money to preserve fish habitats. Kentucky recently contributed $174,000 to the state's Affordable Housing Trust Fund through unclaimed lottery winnings.

State governments maintain that the voluntary contribution of funds through state lotteries is preferable to increased state sales or income taxes, and the residents of states using the lottery system tend to support this. For example, in a recent survey, 59 percent of Alabama residents said they supported their state's lottery. This support increased to 67 percent when people knew the money was being directed toward college scholarships.

The gaming industry has also benefited some of the nation's poorest citizens: Native Americans. The U.S. Supreme Court ruled in 1988 that states could not tax the revenues earned by gambling on Native American reservations. Many tribes have taken advantage of this ruling and opened casinos on their reservations. There are now 298 gaming facilities on reservations in 31 states. From 1988 to 2008, tribal gaming increased from $212 million to $26.5 billion. Many Native Americans moved from a life of poverty to a life of prosperity.

Although there are many advantages to legalized gambling, there has also been a good deal of criticism of state-supported gambling. As states increase their support of state lotteries, they seem to encourage commercial gambling in all its forms. About 50 percent of the U.S. population plays the lottery, according to a study by the University of Chicago. This trend has led to an increase in **compulsive** gambling. More than 5 million Americans suffer from gambling addiction. Those most at risk of becoming addicted include the poor (people earning less than $25,000 a year), young people between 12 and 18 years old, and women over the age of 50—known as "escape gamblers"—who are looking for some **diversion**. Some will try to recover in **rehab** centers; others will even end up homeless. The promise of winning **big bucks** has created big problems.

A further argument against legalized gambling is that not all Native Americans have benefited from their status in the casino industry. Only 200 of the 562 federally registered tribes have casino-style operations. And the majority of reservation casinos cannot make large profits because of their geographic isolation. Moreover, many Native Americans have become addicted to gambling as the gaming industry has taken hold of their communities.

Perhaps the most important concern is the moral issue of legalized gambling. The lottery is the only form of gambling that is essentially a government monopoly. Critics ask whether gambling is a proper function of government. Should the government be the **spokesman** for the expansion of gambling? Critics say state advertising of lotto emphasizes luck over hard work, instant happiness over careful planning, and entertainment over savings. The traditional **work ethic** is being undercut by the **pipe dream** of striking it rich, and this is sending confusing messages to young people.

Congress recently created a **commission** to conduct a comprehensive legal and factual study of the social and economic impacts of gambling in the United States. After two years of study, the commission recommended an end to the expansion of legalized gambling and a ban on Internet gambling. Some feel this will severely hurt the gambling industry. Others fear that it is not enough and are asking the government to **take a tough stand** against gambling.

A. VOCABULARY

Look at the boldfaced words and phrases in the Background Reading. Try to determine their meanings from the context. Write a synonym or your own definition of each boldfaced word. Compare your synonyms and definitions with those of another student. Use a dictionary if necessary.

1. Until 1964 most forms of gambling were illegal in the United States. Since then, however, more and more states have legalized gambling in order to raise **revenue**. . . . all but five states have now legalized gambling as a solution to their depressed economies.

   _____

2. This trend has led to an increase in **compulsive** gambling. More than 5 million Americans suffer from gambling addiction.

   _____

3. Those most at risk of becoming addicted include . . . women over the age of 50—known as "escape gamblers"—who are looking for some **diversion**.

   _____

4. Some will try to recover in **rehab** centers; others will even end up homeless.

   _____

5. The promise of winning **big bucks** has created big problems.

   _____

6. Critics ask whether gambling is a proper function of government. Should the government be the **spokesman** for the expansion of gambling?

_____

7. The traditional **work ethic** is being undercut by the pipe dream of striking it rich, and this is sending confusing messages to young people.

_____

8. The traditional work ethic is being undercut by the **pipe dream** of striking it rich, and this is sending confusing messages to young people.

_____

9. In 1996, Congress created a **commission** to conduct a comprehensive legal and factual study of the social and economic impacts of gambling in the United States.

_____

10. Some feel this will severely hurt the gambling industry. Others fear that it is not enough and are asking the government to **take a tough stand** against gambling.

_____

B. SUMMARIZING THE ISSUE

Work in small groups. Take notes on the following themes in the Background Reading. What are the arguments in favor of (Pro) and against (Con) legalized gambling?

Consider the arguments in terms of the individual, Native American tribes, and the state government. Summarize the issue.

THEMES	PRO	CON
the individual		
Native American tribes		
the state government		

C. VALUES CLARIFICATION

Work in small groups. Discuss your answers to the questions.

1. How is legalized gambling regarded in other countries? Do you support legalized gambling as a form of entertainment? How do you feel about the situation in the United States?

2. Is the system of state-run lotteries different from other forms of gambling? If so, how? Many people would like to ban lotteries. Do you agree with them? Why?

III. OPINION 1: LISTENING

A. LISTENING FOR THE MAIN IDEA

Read the questions and answers. Listen to the commentary and circle the best answer to each question. Then compare your answers with those of another student.

1. What is happening to some individuals who gamble?
   a. They are becoming homeless.
   b. They are changing their religion.
   c. They are getting addicted to alcohol.

2. What is wrong with state lotteries, according to commentator Joe Loconte?
   a. They limit the citizens who can play.
   b. They encourage people to gamble.
   c. They are regulated by the National Gambling Commission.

B. LISTENING FOR DETAILS

Listen again. Write *T* (true) or *F* (false) for each statement. If a statement is false, change it to make it true. Compare your answers with those of another student. Listen again if necessary.

_____ 1. A national gambling commission is examining the growth of the gambling industry.

_____ 2. Lee Smookler, a gambler, was happily married, and he made a lot of money.

_____ 3. Smookler had always been a religious man.

_____ 4. The International Union of Gospel Missions runs faith-based shelters for addicts.

_____ 5. A study asked 1,100 homeless people about gambling and their homelessness.

_____ 6. A majority of the respondents said that gambling played an important role in their homelessness.

_____ 7. One in five respondents said gambling is addictive.

_____ 8. Many shelter clients believe they can make a lot of money gambling.

_____ 9. Poor people tend to spend the most on lotto.

_____10. State treasuries depend on the revenue from lotteries.

_____11. The states may not spend their budget on advertising lotteries.

_____12. Unlike Smookler, Harvard Professor Sandell supports state lotteries.

C. TEXT COMPLETION AND DISCRETE LISTENING

Read the commentary. Fill in the missing words. Then listen again to check your answers. If your answers differ from the commentary, ask your teacher if they are acceptable alternatives.

Introduction

A national gambling _____ is holding meetings around the country
                              1

to examine the _____ of the gambling industry in the U.S. For the
                        2

past two days, they've been in Boston. Commentator Joe Loconte says he hopes the

commission takes a _____ stand on the issue of state lotteries.
                              3

Commentary

Don't try to tell Lee Smookler that gambling is a harmless _____.
                                                                      4

Smookler traded in a happy marriage and successful business for a shot at the big

bucks in Atlantic City. He became a _____ gambler and soon found
                                              5

himself dazed, broke, and _____ on the boardwalk—desperate for
                                    6

_____ change to buy even a cup of coffee.
        7

    Smookler eventually found his way into a rescue mission, where he entered a

rehab program and underwent a Christian _____. Today he's a
                                                      8

_____ for the International Union of Gospel Missions, the nation's
                9

largest association of faith-based shelters. Says Smookler, "The gambling-addicted

man stumbling into a _____ is just as sick as the person addicted to
                     10

_____ or drugs."
        11

That's no exaggeration. The greater accessibility of gambling, from

_____ to electronic poker to lotteries, seems to be turning more and
        12

more lives _____ down. In the first study of its kind, 1,100 clients
           13

from shelters around the country were asked whether gambling played a

_____ role in their homelessness. Nearly one in five said "yes."
        14

Equally troubling, about 86 percent of the respondents said gambling, including

_____, is addictive.
        15

Reverend Steven Berger, executive director of the Gospel Missions, which

_____ the survey, says lotteries and casinos are creating a new
        16

generation of homeless _____. Berger's group took the survey in
                       17

response to increasing reports that shelter clients had been captivated by the

gambling _____ dream.
         18

U.S. Senator Dan Coats says he _____ to make sure the report
                               19

gets into the hands of the National Gambling Commission. At the commission

meeting in Boston, one topic of discussion is the social _____ of
                                                         20

state lotteries. Commission members won't need to look far for

_____.
        21

In Massachusetts, the state's largest _____ treatment center for
                                      22

gamblers reports that lottery players make up 40 percent of its patients. And

according to the *Boston Globe*, the big spenders on lotto are those who can least

_____ it—the poor.
        23

It's one thing for individuals to get _____ on gambling. It's quite

another for state treasuries. Many are addicted to lottery _____ and

are waging slick campaigns to _____ their citizens to ante up. Last

year, states spent upwards of $500 million on advertising their lotteries. That's the

state telling its citizens they need to _____.

Harvard professor of government Michael Sandell calls that "civic corruption–

a policy at odds with the _____ of work, sacrifice, and the moral

responsibility that _____ democratic life." Smookler calls it

"spiritual corruption," one that leads to a shattering of the human spirit.

If members of the gambling commission can't all agree with that assessment,

then, with all respect, let's shuffle the deck and send the _____ home.

IV. OPINION 2: READING

A. READING FOR THE MAIN IDEA

Read the article on the next page. Then do the following activities.

1. Underline the thesis statement, which states the main idea of the article. In
    which paragraph does the writer make his point of view clear?

    _____

2. The title of the article introduces the main idea of the article. Write a new
    title with different words but similar meaning.

    _____

Sure There's a Price, but It Pays to Play

by Ronald Grover

In the early '70s, Atlantic City was a seaside resort on the skids[1]. Then, in 1976, a state referendum authorized casinos on the boardwalk that once featured roller coasters and diving horses. Today, slot-pulling[2] grandmas troop daily into its 14 casinos and drop their share of the $4 billion that the city's casinos rake in each year. An estimated one-third of A.C.'s 38,000 residents work in casinos, and more than 2,000 of them live in apartments paid for by casino taxes.

But there's a yang to this yin[3]. Atlantic County has the most **bankruptcies** in the country, according to New Jersey credit consultants SMR Research Corp.

The question of whether gambling is good for the country is as vexing as it is confusing. On the one hand, **scores** of cities have jump-started economic-development efforts by inviting in gambling palaces, riverboat casinos, and card parlors. Thirty-seven states now offer lotteries that take in $15 billion a year, with a healthy chunk going to education and other worthwhile programs. But "nothing about gaming is as easy as it might look," says Rutgers University Dean of Business Milton Leontiades, who predicts Atlantic City will likely add 20,000 more jobs by 2002, when three new casinos will be built. "For every winner, there's a loser."

Still, the economic benefits of gambling make a powerful argument. Casinos in America employ more than 700,000 people both directly and indirectly, according to a report for the American Gaming Association, a casino **lobbying** group. They funnel $21 billion into the economy through wages and pay out $3 billion annually in state, federal, and local taxes. Gambling directly creates 13 jobs for every $1 million in revenues, the report says, **outpacing** such hot-growth industries as cellular phones and cable TV. "A new casino . . . placed in a market that is not already **saturated**, will **yield** economic benefits on net to its host economy," says a report by Adam Rose, a Pennsylvania State University economist. Rose assessed more than 100 studies by economists who examined the **impact** of gambling on their regions.

The downside is problem gamblers, who are more likely to be unemployed, arrested, divorced, and have more mental-health problems than non-gamblers, according to a new study by the National Opinion Research Center at the University of Chicago. All told, gambling costs society $5 billion a year in medical treatment, jobless benefits, and incarceration[4].

And the casino industry has a dirty little secret that the Rose report **alluded** to: As gambling becomes more **pervasive**, its economic benefits are **diluted**. For every job that the casino industry creates for Shreveport, Louisiana or Hammond, Indiana, it likely loses one from somewhere else.

But when managed properly, gambling can lift workers besides those who find gaming jobs. In Detroit, says Glenn Schaeffer, president of Las Vegas-based Circus Circus Enterprises Inc., banks have started to advertise higher-than-normal wages to compete with the pay at three new casinos. "There's nothing like folks with good-paying jobs to help the economy," he says.

In the end, that might be gambling's trump card. The benefits of feeding coins to a slot machine are hardly universal. Many Indians living on reservations that have won the right to operate casinos are still poor. Economic growth can **stall** when too many games are chasing too few bettors. And compulsive gambling is a social problem of significant proportions. But take a look at Las Vegas, where the unemployment rate is below 3%, the state budget is almost always in surplus, and there are no personal income taxes. In the world of economic development, that's snake eyes[5]. ■

---

[1]*on the skids*: failing
[2]*slot-pulling*: pulling levers on gambling machines
[3]*a yang to this yin*: another side to this story

[4]*incarceration*: putting criminals in jail
[5]*snake eyes*: a winner (from gambling with dice)

B. READING FOR DETAILS

Read the points made in the article. Some of them support the author's thesis, whereas others are points of concession (that is, facts or details that may be true but that do not support the author's main point of view). Review the article. Check the points that support the author's point of view. Compare your answers with those of another student.

❑   1. More than 2,000 Atlantic City residents live in apartments paid for by casino taxes.

❑   2. Atlantic City has the most bankruptcies in the country.

❑   3. Scores of cities have jump-started economic-development efforts through gambling.

❑   4. Thirty-seven states use lottery money for education and other worthwhile programs.

❑   5. Atlantic City will likely add 20,000 more jobs by 2002.

❑   6. American casinos employ more than 700,000 people.

❑   7. Casinos in America pay out $3 billion annually in taxes.

❑   8. Gambling costs society $5 billion a year in medical treatment, jobless benefits, and incarceration.

❑   9. As gambling becomes more pervasive, its economic benefits are diluted.

❑ 10. For every job created by the casino industry, another is likely lost from somewhere else.

❑ 11. In Detroit, banks have started to advertise higher-than-normal wages to compete with the pay at three casinos.

❑ 12. Many Native Americans who have won the right to operate casinos are still poor.

❑ 13. Economic growth can stall when there are too many casinos for the number of players.

❑ 14. In Las Vegas, the unemployment rate is below 3 percent.

❑ 15. There are no personal income taxes in Las Vegas.

Look at the boldfaced words in the editorial. Try to determine their meanings from the context. Complete the following sentences to show you understand the meanings of the boldfaced words. Compare your sentences with those of another student. Use a dictionary if necessary.

1. When a business experiences **bankruptcy**, it _____

   _____.

2. Helen had **scores** of friends, so when she gave parties there were usually

   _____.

3. When **lobbying** politicians, the American Gaming Association probably

   _____.

4. Today technological advancements seem to be **outpacing** _____

   _____.

5. If the market is **saturated** with casinos in a particular area, then _____

   _____.

6. If legalized gambling **yields** economic benefits to state governments,

   _____.

7. A positive **impact** of lotteries is that they _____, while

   a negative **impact** of lotteries is that they _____.

8. The gambler only **alluded** to the fact that he had lost most of his savings,

   so his family _____

   _____.

9. Lotteries have become more **pervasive** in the United States. In fact, _____

   _____.

10. If an alcoholic drink has been **diluted**, it has probably _____

   _____.

11. If the casino industry on Native American reservations **stalls**, it is because

   _____.

V. SYNTHESIZING TWO OPINION PIECES

A. DISTINGUISHING OPINIONS

Write a letter to the National Gambling Commission, which is examining the growth of the gambling industry in the United States. Consider the opinion of commentator Joe Loconte and whether you agree with him. Give your opinion as if you were one of following people:

a. the mayor of Atlantic City

b. Milton Leontiades, Rutgers University dean of business

c. Glenn Schaeffer, president of Circus Circus Enterprises

d. a resident of Las Vegas

B. GIVING YOUR OPINION

Work in pairs. Exchange your letter from Part A with a partner. Read the letter. Write a response in which you express your own opinion about what has been written.

C. VOCABULARY REINFORCEMENT: Word Relations

Work in small groups. For each set of words, cross out the word that is *not* related to the other three. Compare your answers with those of the students in your group. Discuss how the words in each set are related. Then write a word or phrase in the space below that categorizes the relationship. The first one has been done for you.

1. **diversion**   entertainment   ~~commission~~   amusement

    fun way to pass time
    _____

2. **compulsive**   obsessive   intense   pervasive

    _____

3. **spokesman**   naysayer   advocate   defender

    _____

4. **rehab**   outpatient   incarceration   pipe dream

    _____

5. **revenue**	bucks	bankruptcies	income

_____

6. **ethic**	moral	civic	vexing

_____

7. **scores**	insignificant	many	tons

_____

8. **lobbying**	influencing	outpacing	swaying

_____

9. **saturated**	diluted	full	concentrated

_____

10. **yield**	gain	stall	produce

_____

VI. SPEAKING

A. CASE STUDY: The Mashantucket Pequot Indian Casino

The following reading presents a true case that raises the issue of whether gambling is a legitimate form of entertainment and means for raising revenues. Study the case.

In 1637, the English colonists and other Indian tribes almost entirely wiped out the Pequot Indian tribe, who had been living in the southeastern corner of Connecticut. Later, to pacify the few remaining Pequots, the colonists gave the Indians 3,000 acres of land in that area. But as time went on, the colonists began stealing those acres back. By the early 1970s there were only 214 acres left and just two tribe members still living on the Pequot reservation, both aging women.

Connecticut, like the whole nation, has felt guilty for its treatment of the Indians over the past centuries. Over the years, many laws have been passed as a form of payback to the Indians. In 1983, the Pequots were acknowledged as a legitimate tribe and awarded $900,000. With this money they were able to buy back some of their original land. Then in 1988, the U.S. Congress passed the Indian Gaming Regulatory Act, which required states to negotiate agreements in good faith with federally recognized tribes who wanted to conduct gambling on their reservations. After several legal battles, the Pequots won their right to open a casino.

(continued)

In 1992, the Pequot tribe opened its Foxwoods casino. Today, Foxwoods is the second largest and most profitable casino in the world. This is largely due to the fact that it is conveniently placed within 100 miles of 10 percent of the U.S. population, at about an equal distance from New York City and Boston. Foxwoods has nearly 7,000 slot machines, 380 gaming tables, and several hotels, restaurants, lounges, and shops. Its annual revenues are upwards of $1 billion.

The businesses the Pequots have brought to the area have improved Connecticut's economy. Foxwoods is one of the state's largest employers. Moreover, the state receives 25 percent of the money made by all the slot machines, which represents over $2.6 billion since Foxwoods opened in 1992.

By 2008, there were approximately 800 to 900 members of the Pequot tribe, many of whom are only marginally Pequot (one-sixteenth part Pequot blood is the minimum qualification). If a person qualifies, he or she gets housing assistance, training and employment, free health care, free child care, and education for the family's children through graduate school. In addition, as a Pequot, a person is entitled to part ownership of the casino and other tribal businesses. It is not surprising that the tribe gets as many as 50 calls a month from people claiming to have a distant Pequot relative.

The Pequots' success story has not developed without criticism, however. Many argue that the Pequots have been given preferential treatment that has allowed them to create a monopoly. Native American tribes have a special sovereign status in the United States that enables them to create their own legal codes, courts, and constitutions. Therefore, unlike casinos not owned by an Indian nation, Foxwoods is exempt from local real estate taxes and federal income taxes—as is the tribal government. Many people feel this is unfair.

Perhaps those most unhappy are the local residents of small towns surrounding the Pequot reservation. They complain that crowds of people have taken over their once-tranquil communities. Approximately 40,000 guests stream through Foxwoods every day. Traffic is a mess. The roads to Foxwoods are jammed on weekends. A local priest, Charles Spiller, says he has to pray his way out of his driveway each day. In fact, many homes along Route 2, the road leading to the casino, now have "For Sale" signs posted in front of their properties. "We're being pushed out of our way of life," says Andrea Gialluca, who lives a few miles from the casino. "Our environment is changing." Local residents worry about the environmental effects of further development around the casino.

Meanwhile, as local resistance to Foxwoods and the gambling industry grows, the Pequots continue to build and expand. They have built the most expensive and perhaps fastest ferryboat of its size ever built in the United States in order to carry gamblers from New York City to Foxwoods. They have built a museum and research center on their reservation. They have plans to bring an amusement park into the area in the near future as well as to build a casino in Pennsylvania. Some might say that it is now the Pequots who are "colonizing" the acres they almost lost more than 300 years ago.

Prepare for a role play. Read the situation and the roles, and follow the procedure.

The Situation

The Senate Governmental Affairs Committee has appointed a national commission to study the economic and social effects of legalized gambling. Today the commission will discuss, in particular, the Foxwoods casino and how it has affected the local community. The members will meet with key people who have been involved with the casino issue. Foxwoods will serve as a case study for the Committee's recommendations for the future of Native American gaming. The following people will meet to discuss their views, findings, and opinions:

The Roles

1. **The Senate Governmental Affairs Committee members:** The committee has been charged with investigating the pros and cons of legalized gambling. Members are interested in meeting with local members of the community surrounding the Foxwoods casino to find out how the U.S. policy on Native American gaming affects local communities.

2. **Those against Native American gaming:**

   a. White House Representative: She sides with the president, who questions the morality of Native American gaming. He said, "Too often, public officials view gambling as a quick and easy way to raise revenues without focusing on gambling's hidden social, economic, and political costs."

   b. Member of the Christian Coalition: She feels gambling is destroying families and causing more social problems in her community. She has pledged resources to fight legalized gambling.

   c. Donald Trump: He owns a casino in Atlantic City. He is against the special financial treatment given to the tribes.

   d. Andrea Gialluca: She lives a few miles from the casino. She feels residents are being pushed out of their way of life. The environment is changing. Route 2 is backed up all the way to her house with casino-bound traffic.

3. **Those in favor of Native American gaming:**

   a. Alan Bergren: He is city manager of Norwich, Connecticut, and feels Foxwoods has been a godsend. His decaying river town, in which thousands of people had lost their defense industry jobs, is slowly being restored because of revenues brought in by the casino. He sees the Pequots as important benefactors.

   b. Michael Thomas: He has been chairman of the Pequot Tribal Council since November 2002, leading language revitalization among tribal members and touching the lives of 15,000 employees as well as families in the surrounding area. As treasurer, he issued the first-ever treasurer's report to the Mashantucket Pequot people, making tribal government fully transparent. He has watched his people move out of poverty and into prosperity and supports the gambling industry.

   c. Pedro Johnson, chairman of the Foxwoods Development Company Board of Directors: He is a tribal elder who feels operating Foxwoods has given the Pequots invaluable expertise. He supports helping other tribes in the United States develop casinos.

   d. Joey Carter: He has recently learned much about his tribe's history from talking to anthropologists. The casino business has allowed his tribe to come together again and discover their history and culture.

(continued)

The Procedure

1. Form the three groups to plan your position.

2. The commission prepares questions for the participants.

3. Those against Native American gaming summarize and develop their points of view.

4. Those in favor of Native American gaming summarize and develop their points of view.

5. The commission interviews the interested parties, makes a recommendation on Native American gaming, and presents it to the whole group.

B. DISCUSSION QUESTIONS

Work in groups. Discuss your answers to the questions.

1. Do you agree with Lee Smookler's remark in the commentary, "The gambling-addicted man stumbling into a mission is just as sick as the person addicted to booze or drugs"? Is gambling as serious as a physical dependency on alcohol or drugs, or is it different? Have you ever known someone addicted to gambling? If so, describe that person's condition.

2. More employment, higher salaries, and "quality of life" benefits to the local communities are some of the positive results of legalized gambling. Should those states in the United States that have not adopted a lottery system for their state treasuries do so? Or should a reverse trend be initiated, with an emphasis on finding new ways to raise money for the economy? Discuss your opinions.

VII. WRITING

A. GRAMMAR: Adjective Clauses

Notice   Notice the structure of the underlined adjective clauses in these sentences taken from both the commentary and the article:

   a. *Smookler eventually found his way into a rescue mission, **where** he entered a rehab program and underwent a Christian conversion.*

   b. *Reverend Steven Berger, executive director of the Gospel Missions, **which** conducted the survey, says lotteries and casinos are creating a new generation of homeless addicts.*

   c. *And according to the* Boston Globe, *the big spenders on lotto are those **who** can least afford it—the poor.*

d. Harvard professor of government Michael Sandell calls that "civic corruption," a policy at odds with the ethic of work, sacrifice, and the moral responsibility ***that*** *sustains democratic life*.

e. But "nothing about gaming is as easy as it might look," says Rutgers University Dean of Business Milton Leontiades, ***who*** *predicts Atlantic City will likely add 20,000 more jobs by 2002*, ***when*** *three new casinos will be built*.

Discuss what each of the relative pronouns and relative adverbs (in boldface) refers to in each clause. Which of the adjective clauses are introduced by a comma and which are not? Can you explain why?

Explanation   Like adjectives, adjective clauses give us information about nouns. They can be used effectively to combine two simple ideas into one, making sentences more complex and sophisticated.

Adjective clauses are subordinate clauses that are linked by the relative pronouns (*who, whom, that, which, whose*) or the relative adverbs for time and place (*when* and *where*).

The examples above illustrate two types of adjective clauses: restrictive and nonrestrictive. In the adjective clauses in *c* and *d*, the information that follows the relative pronoun cannot be taken out of the sentence. It is necessary in order to identify the meaning of the noun in the sentence. In these restrictive adjective clauses, the clause is not separated by commas.

In the adjective clauses in *a*, *b*, and *e*, however, the information that follows the relative pronoun can be taken out of the sentence; it provides extra information. It is not necessary to identify or explain the meaning of the noun in the sentence. In these nonrestrictive adjective clauses, the clause is separated by commas.

Notice that you do not use the relative pronoun *that* in nonrestrictive adjective clauses; instead, use *who* to describe a person or *which* to describe a thing, such as in example *b* and in the first clause in example *e*.

Exercise

Complete the sentences with the correct relative pronoun or adverb. Add commas where necessary. The first one has been done for you.

1. Lee Smookler _____, who _____ traded in a happy marriage and successful business for a shot at the big bucks in Atlantic City, became a compulsive gambler.

2. A form of entertainment _____ is turning more and more lives upside down is legalized gambling.

3. In Boston _____ the National Gambling Commission is meeting, one topic of discussion is the social impact of state lotteries.

4. In the largest outpatient treatment center in Massachusetts, the percentage

   of outpatients _____ play lotto is 40.

5. The early 1970s was a time _____ Atlantic City was on
   the skids.

6. A market _____ is not already saturated will yield economic
   benefits to its host economy.

7. An American city _____ the unemployment rate is below

   3 percent and _____ the state budget is almost always in
   surplus is Las Vegas.

8. Many Native Americans _____ reservations operate casinos
   are still poor.

B. WRITING STYLE: Idioms

Notice   Notice the way the writers of the commentary and article make frequent use of
idiomatic phrases expressing their opinions on the gambling industry. Can you
find any of these phrases? What do you think they mean?

Explanation   Idioms are informal phrases that help make a language come alive. They are quite
common in English but may be difficult to understand because they consist of a
group of words that has a special meaning. Knowing the meaning of the individual
words in an idiom will not necessarily help a reader understand the idiom's
meaning.

   Idioms are, in fact, at the heart of the English language, because many of the words
that form them come from Old English. There are more than 10,000 idioms in the
English language, and it is impossible to learn them all. However, it is possible to learn
how to understand them. One way is to use the context clues of the sentence to help
determine an idiom's meaning. If the sentence context is not enough, the sentences
before and after the sentence containing the idiom may provide helpful clues.

Exercise 1

**Read the following sentences from the commentary and the article. Return to the
commentary and article and reread the sentences that come before and after these
sentences. Circle the letter of the correct meaning of the boldfaced idiom.**

1. Commentator Joe Loconte says he hopes the commission **takes a tough
   stand on** the issue of state lotteries.
   a. changes its position on
   b. makes a difficult choice about
   c. maintains a high standard on

2. Smookler traded in a happy marriage and successful business for **a shot at** the big bucks in Atlantic City.
   a. a chance for
   b. a fight for
   c. a loss of

3. The greater accessibility of gambling, from casinos to electronic poker to lotteries, seems to be turning more and more **lives upside down**.
   a. reversing people's earnings
   b. dramatically changing people's lives
   c. increasing people's free time

4. It's one thing for individuals to **get hooked on** gambling.
   a. feel attracted to
   b. lose money with
   c. become addicted to

5. Many are addicted to lottery revenue and are waging slick campaigns to convince their citizens to **ante up**.
   a. pay
   b. get help
   c. win

6. Harvard professor of government Michael Sandell calls that "civic corruption," a policy **at odds with** the ethic of work, sacrifice, and the moral responsibility that sustains democratic life.
   a. in support of
   b. in disagreement with
   c. identical to

7. If members of the gambling commission can't all agree with that assessment, then, with all respect, let's **shuffle the deck** and send the losers home.
   a. end the job of the commission
   b. cut the cost of the commission
   c. get new people on the commission

8. In the early '70s, Atlantic City was a seaside resort **on the skids**.
   a. failing
   b. growing
   c. maintaining

9. Today, slot-pulling grandmas troop daily into its 14 casinos and **drop their share** of the $4 billion that the city's casinos rake in each year.
   a. divide their portion
   b. contribute their portion
   c. win their portion

10. Today, slot-pulling grandmas troop daily into its 14 casinos and drop their share of the $4 billion that the city's casinos **rake in** each year.
    a. lose
    b. pay
    c. collect

Exercise 2

Read the following true story about a man addicted to the lottery. Fill in the blanks with an appropriate idiom from the box. Use the context of the text to help you. Be sure to use the correct verb or pronoun form.

ante up	on the skids	take a shot at
drop (one's) share	rake in	take a tough stand on
hooked on	shuffle the deck	turn (one's) life upside down

Several years ago, Robert Desmond summoned his children around him to tell them his heartbreaking news: He was _____, unable to pay his bills
                                                1
or even light his house. His children, shocked by their father's financial condition, couldn't understand what had _____. But they promised they
                                                2
would work together to help him straighten out his finances.

Days later, however, Desmond's daughter discovered the reason for their father's demise. She found spent lotto tickets lying around his house and car. Her father was _____ the lottery and had cashed in his pension and sold
              3
family possessions in order to play lotto! Desmond's daughter _____
                                                4
her father's addiction. She sold the family house to pay her father's debts.

Desmond's story is not uncommon. Many average, middle-class Americans find themselves losing control as they _____ into the earnings of their
                                    5
state's lottery. The state of Massachusetts, whose lottery _____
                                                6
upwards of $809 million last year, recently introduced the $10 ticket, encouraging its citizens to _____ and play for more. It seems that many people are
              7

willing to _____ winning, despite the low odds. In fact, the tickets are
                    8

selling faster than had been expected—at an average rate of 358,101 a day.

Many people who are against gambling feel that government commissions are

too pro-gambling. Voters might _____ and elect new, anti-gambling
                                        9

voices in government as well.

C. ESSAY QUESTIONS

Write an essay on one of the numbered topics. Use ideas, vocabulary, and writing techniques from this unit. Try to incorporate the following:

- an introductory paragraph that presents both sides of the argument and clearly states your thesis

- paragraphs (at least three) that develop your argument with supporting evidence

- a conclusion that reinforces the position you have taken and ends with a new idea (a warning, prediction, value judgment) that has not been mentioned before

1. In the commentary, Harvard professor Michael Sandell is quoted as saying that advertising state lotteries is "civic corruption, a policy at odds with the ethic of work, sacrifice, and moral responsibility that sustains democratic life." Richard Moran, a professor of sociology and criminology, supports Sandell's view. He states: "The main problem with the lottery is that it undermines the work ethic by severing the relationship between individual effort and financial reward."

   Do you believe that people can maintain a work ethic and moral responsibility while playing games of chance? Write an essay in which you express your opinion.

2. Gambling is practiced all over the world, though policies surrounding it can differ greatly. Compare and contrast the gambling policies of the United States with those of another country that you know well. Write an essay in which you compare and contrast the two policies.

Alternative Energy

John Cole

I. ANTICIPATING THE ISSUE

Discuss your answers to the questions.

1. Look at the title. Look at the cartoon. What do you think the issue of this unit will be?

2. What is the message or humor of the cartoon?

3. What do you know about developments in alternative energy? What are the pros and cons?

Read the text.

The **procurement** of oil is becoming more costly and more political. Because of this and the environmental consequences of our fuel-based economy, the world has **set** its **sights on** developing alternative energy sources. It is clear that we need to create cleaner energy sources for the twenty-first century. But what will help **wean** us **off** of our dependence on fossil fuels?

Wind is one source of energy that makes sense. It is **abundant**: It exists in most areas of the world, is free, and is easy to collect. In addition, wind-generated electricity is free of any emissions. For these reasons, the **harnessing** of wind energy makes sense in helping us reduce our dependence on oil and other fossil fuels, like coal and natural gas. However, wind may not be the best alternative energy solution for some: Wind does not blow constantly, the cost of setting up wind turbines is high, the noise produced by rotor blades in wind power can be loud and disturbing, and many people feel that wind turbines destroy the natural views of coastlines where they are typically built.

The cost of solar power is **commensurate with** that of wind energy. It is also nonpolluting. It needs no fuel and can be set up easily with the use of large flat panels made up of individual solar cells. These cells collect sunlight and convert it into electricity. However, like wind power, solar power is very expensive. Some solar cells cost a great deal compared to the amount of electricity they will produce in their lifetime. Moreover, solar power can be close to useless in climates that are not sunny.

Many scientists support the development of hydrogen as an energy source to replace oil. It is a "green" source of energy because its only **byproduct** is water. Changing from fossil fuels to hydrogen could dramatically reduce air pollution, lower dependence on oil, and reduce the build-up of greenhouse gases. The problem is that pollution-free sources of hydrogen are not likely to be practical or affordable for decades. Hydrogen is not a readily accessible energy source like wind and the sun. It is bound up in molecules like water, so it is expensive and energy-intensive to produce. In fact, it costs four times as much as gasoline to deliver in a usable form. Researchers from the Massachusetts Institute of Technology (MIT) recently **weighed in** on the proposal to shift to a hydrogen-based economy. They said that, despite the aggressive research on hydrogen fuel, engines powered by gasoline will still be the best option for automobiles in the immediate future.

Biofuels are still another source of alternative energy that has developed in recent years. Farmers around the world have **marshaled** their crops of corn, palm oil, sugar cane, and soybeans for fuel production. These biofuels have been embraced by the global community because, unlike fossil fuels, which pollute, they are "carbon-neutral." In other words, even though carbon is released when a biofuel is burned, a similar amount of carbon is absorbed from the atmosphere as the crops grow. In this way, biofuels are considered **sustainable**. Yet, it has recently become clear that the overall environmental impact of biofuels could be even worse than that of petroleum. In fact, Oxfam estimated that by the year 2020, the European Union's target for biofuel use could **usher in** carbon emissions that are

70 times higher than what we produce today. In addition, the impact of biofuels on rising food prices is affecting the poor throughout the world. Currently 800 million people with cars compete with 800 million people with hunger problems. It has been estimated that the amount of grain necessary to fill a 25-gallon tank with ethanol is the same amount necessary to feed one person for a whole year.

So, should we be filling gas tanks instead of stomachs? Is the economic investment of a hydrogen-based economy worth it? Could wind and sun be our energy solutions of the future? These are questions that will have to be answered in the coming years.

A. VOCABULARY

Look at the boldfaced words and phrases in the Background Reading. Try to determine their meanings from the context. Complete the following sentences to show that you understand the meaning of each boldfaced word and phrase. Compare your sentences with those of another student. Use a dictionary if necessary.

1. America's future **procurement** of oil will largely depend on

   _____.

2. Much of the world has **set** its **sights on** the Middle East for

   _____.

3. We will only be **weaned off** our dependence on carbon-based fuels when

   _____.

4. Two natural resources that are **abundant** on the earth are

   _____.

5. The successful **harnessing** of solar power depends on

   _____.

6. The cost of driving vehicles using gasoline is not **commensurate with**

   _____.

7. The worst **byproduct** of driving cars using gasoline

   _____.

8. There used to be much disagreement over whether the earth was warming as a result of human activity, but now most climate scientists have **weighed in,** saying _____.

9. A leader in my country who has **marshaled** support for energy

   independence is _____.

10. Our need to develop more **sustainable** forms of energy comes from the

    fact that

    _____.

11. With third-world countries demanding a greater share of the world's oil

    supply, we have **ushered in**

    _____.

B. SUMMARIZING THE ISSUE

Work in small groups. Take notes on the negative and positive effects of developing the alternative energy sources discussed in the Background Reading.

Positive Effects of Developing Alternative Energy Sources	Negative Effects of Developing Alternative Energy Sources
_____	_____
_____	_____
_____	_____
_____	_____

C. VALUES CLARIFICATION

Work in groups. Discuss your answers to the questions.

1. In your opinion, are there more positive or negative effects in developing alternative fuels? Explain.

2. Which alternative fuel deserves to be supported most by government subsidies?

3. What sources of alternative energy are most supported in your country? Do you think this is a good idea?

III. OPINION 1: LISTENING

A. LISTENING FOR THE MAIN IDEA

Listen to the commentary. Check the statement that best summarizes the commentator's main idea.

❑ 1. A hydrogen economy is not possible, given the constraints of our economy and resources.

❑ 2. A hydrogen economy should be promoted immediately because it has so many promises.

❑ 3. A hydrogen economy is desirable, but it requires a public-private partnership.

B. LISTENING FOR DETAILS

Listen again and answer the questions. For each question, two answers are correct. Cross out the answer that is *not* correct. Compare your answers with those of another student. Listen again if necessary.

1. According to Jeremy Rifkin, who or what needs to be mobilized to wean society off the fossil fuel grid?
   a. financial resources
   b. entrepreneurial talent
   c. government

2. Which reasons does he mention for doing this?
   a. global warming
   b. lack of oil
   c. geopolitical tensions in the Gulf

3. Why is hydrogen so desirable?
   a. It's the most abundant element in the universe.
   b. Its byproducts are no different from those from the industrial revolution.
   c. It will create a new energy revolution.

4. Which comparison is made to the impact hydrogen can have?
   a. oil in the nineteenth century
   b. steam power in the nineteenth century
   c. oil-powered internal combustion engines in the twentieth century

5. How can we create a hydrogen-based economy?
   a. with a 10-year goal
   b. as a collaborative effort
   c. by following California's lead

6. Who has barely weighed in on the promise of hydrogen?
   a. the White House
   b. Congress
   c. research and development committees

7. Who should we enlist?
   a. international laboratories
   b. federal laboratories and universities
   c. industry and civil institutions

8. What should government do to help the hydrogen-based economy develop?
   a. provide tax credits
   b. purchase hydrogen fuel cell vehicles
   c. make commercial products

9. What concerns does Rifkin have about hydrogen?
   a. how we can afford it
   b. the possible lost opportunity for a sustainable energy
   c. the government's support so far

C. TEXT COMPLETION AND DISCRETE LISTENING

Read the commentary. Fill in the missing suffixes for each adjective. Then listen again to check your answers.

Introduction
Commentator Jeremy Rifkin is author of *The Hydrogen Economy*. He says private companies won't be able to realize a vision of an economy free of fossil fuels on their own.

Commentary

It's clear: We need to mobilize the financ_____ resources, entrepreneur_____
                                          1   **2**

talent and scientif_____ know-how of the world to wean society off the fossil
                   3

fuel grid. The reasons are obvious: global warming, the high price of oil, and the

growing geopolitic_____ tensions in the Persian Gulf.
                  4

Hydrogen is the light_____ and most abundant element in the universe.
                     5

Scientists call it the "forever fuel" because it never runs out. And when hydrogen's

us_____ to produce power, the only byproducts are pure water and heat.
  6

Hydrogen-power_____ fuel cells will usher in a third industr_____
7   8
revolution. Its impact will be as profound as the harnessing of coal and steam

power in the nineteenth century and the oil-power_____ intern_____
9   10
combustion engine in the twentieth century.

   But how do we create a hydrogen-based economy? A hydrogen energy regime

requires a public-private partnership on a grand scale, the kind we marshaled in

the Apollo space program when the U.S. set its sights on landing a man on the

moon in 10 years. The space program was a collaborat_____ effort, and it
11
worked. Now we should set an equally ambiti_____ goal of creating a fully
12
integrat_____ hydrogen economy by 2030. California has already charged
13
ahead with a program to become the first fully operation_____ hydrogen
14
economy in the United States. Several other states are following California's lead.

   The problem is the White House and Congress have barely weighed in. What's

requir_____ is a massive research and development commitment at the
15
feder_____ level, in the order of billions of dollars spread out over the next
16
few decades. We should enlist the nation's feder_____ laboratories and
17
universities in every aspect of the effort, along with industry and civil institutions.

We should enact legislation at both the feder_____ and state levels to provide
18
spec_____ tax credits and other incentives to encourage start-up companies to
19
stay in the field and establish_____ companies to enter the field. The
20
feder_____ government and states should purchase hydrogen fuel cell cars,
21
buses, and trucks for government fleets as well as station_____ fuel cells for
22
government buildings and facilities. Early procurement will help reduce costs and

create economies of scale to stimulate broad commerc_____ and consumer
23
demand.

All of this is just the beginning. The key is to make a nation_____
24
commitment to a new energy regime commensurate with the magnitude of the
task at hand. For those who question whether we can afford all this, perhaps we
should turn the question around and ask: How do we even begin to calculate the
lost opportunity if we say no to a sustain_____ energy future and a third
25
industr_____ revolution?
26

Now work with a partner and do the following:
- Place each adjective into a suffix category in the chart.
- Put a stress mark over the stressed syllable.
- Add one or two of your own examples in each category.
- Discuss the following questions:
  a. Does the syllable stress change from the base form of the word?
  b. Can you make any generalizations about stress change from these
     suffix endings?

SUFFIX	MEANING	EXAMPLE(S) FROM COMMENTARY	MY EXAMPLE(S)
-able	capable of being		
-al	relating to		
-ary	having a particular quality		
-ed	completedness (from passive verb form)		
-est	most of something (superlative)		
-ial	relating to		
-ic	relating to		
-ive	able to do something		
-ous	characterized by; having quality of		

A. READING FOR THE MAIN IDEAS

Read the editorial. Check the statements that best summarize the author's main ideas.

- ❑ 1. Biofuels will reduce global warming.
- ❑ 2. Biofuel emissions are more serious than gasoline emissions.
- ❑ 3. Biofuels will destroy ecosystems.
- ❑ 4. Biofuels will close markets to individual farmers.
- ❑ 5. Biofuels will solve the world hunger problem.
- ❑ 6. The biofuel industry needs more regulations.

Biofuel Myths
by Eric Holt-Giménez

The term "biofuels" suggests **renewable** abundance: clean, green, sustainable assurance about technology and progress. This pure image allows industry, politicians, the World Bank, the United Nations, and even the International Panel on Climate Change to present fuels made from corn, sugarcane, soy, and other crops as the next step in a smooth transition from peak oil to a yet-to-be-defined renewable fuel economy.

But in reality, biofuel draws its power from **cornucopian** myths and directs our attention away from economic interests that would benefit from the transition, while avoiding discussion of the growing North-South food and energy imbalance.

They **obscure** the political-economic relationships between land, people, resources, and food, and fail to help us understand the profound consequences of the industrial transformation of our food and fuel systems. "Agro-fuels" better describes the industrial interests behind the transformation, and is the term most widely used in the global South.

Industrialized countries started the biofuels boom by demanding ambitious renewable-fuel targets. These fuels are to provide 10 percent of Europe's transport power by 2020. The United States wants 35 billion gallons a year.

These targets far exceed the agricultural capacities of the industrial North. Europe would need to plant 70 percent of its farmland with fuel crops. The entire corn and soy harvest of the United States would need to be processed as ethanol and biodiesel. Converting most **arable** land to fuel crops would destroy the food systems of the North, so the Organisation of Economic Cooperation and Development countries are looking to the South to meet demand.

The rapid capitalization and concentration of power within the biofuels industry is extreme. Over the past three years, venture capital investment in biofuels has increased by 800 percent. Private investment is **swamping** public research institutions.

Behind the scenes, under the noses of most national antitrust laws, giant oil, grain, auto, and genetic engineering corporations are forming partnerships, and they are **consolidating** the research, production, processing, and distribution chains of food and fuel systems under one industrial roof.

Biofuel champions assure us that because fuel crops are renewable, they are environment-friendly, can reduce global warming, and will foster rural development. But the tremendous market power of biofuel corporations, coupled with the poor political will of governments to regulate their activities, make this unlikely. We need a public enquiry into the myths:

Biofuels are clean and green.
Because photosynthesis performed by fuel crops removes greenhouse gases from the atmosphere and can reduce fossil fuel consumption, we are told they are green. But when the full life cycle of biofuels is considered, from land clearing to consumption, the moderate emission savings are outweighed by far greater **emissions** from deforestation, burning, **peat** drainage, cultivation, and soil-carbon losses.

Every ton of palm oil generates 33 tons of carbon dioxide emissions—10 times more than petroleum. Tropical forests cleared for sugar cane ethanol emit 50 percent more greenhouse gases than the production and use of the same amount of gasoline.

Biofuels will not result in deforestation.
Proponents of biofuels argue that fuel crops planted on ecologically degraded lands will improve rather than destroy the environment. Perhaps the government of Brazil had this in mind when it reclassified some 200 million **hectares** of dry-tropical forests, grassland, and marshes as degraded and **apt** for cultivation.

In reality, these are the biodiverse ecosystems of the Atlantic Forest, the Cerrado, and the Pantanal, occupied by indigenous people, subsistence farmers, and extensive cattle ranches. The introduction of agrofuel plantations will push these communities to the agricultural frontier of the Amazon, where the devastating patterns of deforestation are well known.

Soybeans supply 40 percent of Brazil's biofuels. NASA has correlated their market price with the destruction of the Amazon rainforest—currently at nearly 325,000 hectares a year.

Biofuels will bring rural development.
In the tropics, 100 hectares dedicated to family farming generates 35 jobs. Oil-palm and sugarcane provide 10 jobs, eucalyptus two, and soybeans a scant half-job per 100 hectares, all poorly paid.

Until recently, biofuels supplied primarily local and sub-regional markets. Even in the United States, most ethanol plants were small and farmer-owned. With the boom, big industry is moving in, centralizing operations and creating **gargantuan** economies of scale.

Biofuels producers will be dependent on a cabal[1] of companies for their seed, inputs, services, processing, and sale. They are not likely to receive many benefits. Small holders will be forced out of the market and off the land. Hundreds of thousands have already been displaced by the soybean plantations in the "Republic of Soy," a 50-million hectare area in southern Brazil, northern Argentina, Paraguay, and eastern Bolivia.

Biofuels will not cause hunger.
Hunger results not from **scarcity**, but poverty. The world's poorest already spend 50 to 80 percent of household income on food. They suffer when high fuel prices push up food prices. Now, because food and fuel crops compete for land and resources, both increase the price of land and water.

The International Food Policy Research Institute has estimated that the price of basic **staples** will increase 26 to 135 percent by 2020. Caloric consumption declines as price rises by a ratio of 1:2.

Limits must be placed on the biofuels industry. The North cannot shift the burden of overconsumption to the South because the tropics have more sunlight, rain, and arable land. If biofuels are to be forest- and food-friendly, the grain, cane, and palm oil industries need to be regulated, and not **piecemeal**.

Strong, enforceable standards based on limiting land planted for biofuels are urgently needed, as are antitrust laws powerful enough to prevent the corporate concentration of market power in the industry. Sustainable benefits to the countryside will only **accrue** if biofuels are a complement to plans for sustainable rural development, not the centerpiece.

A global **moratorium** on the expansion of biofuels is needed to develop regulatory structures and foster conservation and development alternatives to the transition. We need the time to make a better transition to food and fuel sovereignty. ∎

Originally published in the *International Herald Tribune*, July 10, 2007. Copyright ©2007 by the *International Herald Tribune*. Reprinted by permission.

---

[1]*cabal*: conspiratorial group of plotters

B. READING FOR DETAILS

Read the statements. Decide whether they are _T_ (true) or _F_ (false), based on the opinions of the author.

_____ 1. Biofuels allow a smooth transition from oil to renewable fuel.

_____ 2. There is a growing problem with the balance of food and energy between the North and South.

_____ 3. The industrial transformation of our food and fuel systems is of concern.

_____ 4. "Agro-fuels" are a positive goal for the future.

_____ 5. The renewable-fuel targets of industrialized countries are too ambitious.

_____ 6. Conversion of arable land to fuel crops should happen in the South rather than in the North.

_____ 7. Private investment is needed in public research institutions.

_____ 8. Corporate partnerships are helpful as they consolidate the research of biofuels.

_____ 9. Governments have poor political will to regulate fuel crops.

_____ 10. The photosynthesis of fuel crops helps reduce the greenhouse gases from the atmosphere.

_____ 11. The production of palm oil and sugar cane ethanol emit more greenhouse gases than the production of gasoline.

_____ 12. The government of Brazil made a good decision when it reclassified its 200 million hectares for cultivation.

_____ 13. Indigenous people should move more of their agriculture toward the Amazon.

_____ 14. More soybeans should be grown for biofuels in Brazil.

_____ 15. Farmer-owned ethanol plants are better than big industry plants.

_____ 16. The soybean plantations destroy small subsistence farming.

_____ 17. The world's poorest spend too much of their income on food.

_____ 18. The South should help solve the North's problem of overconsumption.

_____ 19. We need more time to produce biofuels.

C. WORD SEARCH

Write the boldfaced words from the editorial next to the following words or phrases that have a similar meaning.

Nouns

1. _____: waste substances released into the air or water

2. _____: units of measurement of land (10,000 square meters)

3. _____: a small, inadequate amount

4. _____: consumer goods that are bought often and consumed routinely (such as bread, milk, sugar)

5. _____: an agreed suspension of activity

Adjectives

6. _____: made from partially carbonized vegetable matter saturated with water

7. _____: made from fuel resources from the environment such as wind, water, or the sun

8. _____: suitable for producing crops

9. _____: expressing belief in continued progress without harmful consequences

10. _____: naturally disposed toward

11. _____: huge; gigantic

12. _____: gradually; in stages

Verbs

13. _____: cover over; hide

14. _____: filling quickly beyond capacity

15. _____: grow by addition

16. _____: combining two or more things to make one thing that is more effective

A. DISTINGUISHING OPINIONS

In his commentary, Jeremy Rifkin discusses positive views of alternative energy by focusing on hydrogen. In his editorial, Eric Holt-Giménez discusses negative views of alternative energy by focusing on biofuels. Although these types of alternative energy are different, their developments bring up common issues.

For each issue, take notes on what each person says.

ISSUES	RIFKIN: (OPINION 1)	HOLT-GIMÉNEZ: (OPINION 2)
Transition from fossil fuels to alternative energy		
Economic cost of alternative energy		
Impact of alternative energy on the environment		
Government responsibility in dealing with alternative energy		

B. GIVING YOUR OPINION

Work in groups. Discuss your answers to the following questions:

1. What arguments could be made against Rifkin's positive views of hydrogen? What arguments could be made against Holt-Giménez's negative views of biofuels?

2. Do you tend to favor the views of Rifkin or Holt-Giménez? Do you have more hopes or doubts about the promises of alternative energy sources? Why?

Read the sentences. Cross out the one phrase in parentheses that does not make sense. Use your understanding of the boldfaced vocabulary to make your choice.

1. Americans have had a tough time being **weaned off** their heavy use of petroleum because (biofuels have become so popular / they refuse to give up their SUVs / changing to renewable energy is an expensive process).

2. The production of biofuels may be **commensurate with** an increase in global warming in that (farmers will grow crops for fuel instead of food / growing crops for fuel reduces the amount of carbon dioxide released into the atmosphere / clearing more land for biofuel crops causes deforestation).

3. The **procurement** of oil in the future (will be difficult if environmental groups prevent more off-shore drilling / will depend on foreign relations / will control emissions released into the environment).

4. **Sustainable** use of natural resources will require (planting crops on land that is already cleared / cutting down more rainforest / eating foods that are grown locally).

5. Our attempts to make the earth "greener" sometimes **obscure** (the decrease of emissions into the environment / the high costs of switching to alternative energies / the fact that the production of renewable energy sources can be damaging to the environment).

6. Our **cornucopian** views about energy (cause us to believe in science and its ability to come up with new energy solutions / prevent us from making changes in our lifestyle / help us recognize the limitations of the earth).

7. Biofuels are **apt** for an increase in production because (governments give subsidies to farmers so they will grow them / people believe that they are the green alternative to fossil fuels / farmers cannot easily produce them).

8. Because of the **scarcity** of (wind / fossil fuels / arable land) on the planet, a variety of alternative energy sources will be necessary in the future.

9. If our conversion to alternative sources of energy is done in a **piecemeal** fashion, we will (not solve the problem of global warming / make great progress in reducing our dependency on fossil fuels / lose sight of the actual economic and environmental costs).

10. With a **moratorium** on biofuels, (more small farmers will change their crops for ethanol / more time can be spent studying the global effects of biofuel farming / we will increase our dependency on fossil fuels).

VI. SPEAKING

A. CASE STUDY: Brazil's Deforestation

The following presents a true case in Brazil that raises the issue of whether biofuels are a solution to global warming.

Work in small groups. Study the case below, and discuss the issue of biofuels as it is presented. Put yourselves in the position of the Intergovernmental Panel on Climate Change (IPCC), the government body in charge of evaluating relevant scientific, technical, and socioeconomic information, in order to understand the risk of climate change caused by humans. Write a list of proposals for future soybean production in Brazil. Present your conclusions to the rest of the class. Consider the following questions:

- Should Brazil's government subsidize soybean plantations?
- Should there be government subsidies anywhere for biofuel?
- Can alternatives to soybean plantations be found to help Brazil's economy?
- Is legislation necessary? If so, what laws should be passed?
- Do consumers need to change their habits? If so, what can or should consumers do?

It is clear that the burning of fossil fuels has contributed to global warming and climate change. Consequently, nations around the world are looking for energy alternatives. For example, the European Union has the goal of replacing 10 percent of its transport fuel with biofuels by 2020. China is aiming for 15 percent by the same date. The United States has already gone beyond its original plan to double the amount of ethanol used in motor vehicles by 2012. These ambitious goals to convert our energy have created an explosion in demand for biofuels, causing an enormous impact on agriculture around the world. One country where this impact is most severe is Brazil, where there has been a dramatic expansion of soybean plantations. This expansion is driven, directly and indirectly, by biofuel agriculture and is beginning to invade the Amazon rainforest.

One source of the biofuel issue in Brazil is a chain reaction that can be traced to the United States. Today more and more American corn crops are devoted to the production of biofuels. For example, about 25 percent of American corn is now grown to produce ethanol rather than food. Since 2000, the U.S. production of ethanol has increased from 1.6 billion gallons to 6.5 billion gallons. But here is the issue: Because of this rising demand for ethanol, many U.S. farmers have been replacing their soybean fields with corn fields, and this has lowered the world's supply of soybeans and driven up their price.

To respond to the lack of soybeans on the global market, farmers in Brazil have begun to create more soybean plantations. This is having an effect on the Amazon rainforest, one of the most critical ecosystems on the planet. (The Amazon rainforest contains up to one third of the plant and animal species known to humans.) The new soybean plantations are not being planted in the rainforest, but their development is having a serious effect on this critical area. As small farmers and cattle ranchers are displaced from their land to create soybean plantations, they move into the rainforest, cutting trees and clearing land to continue ranching. Over 18,000 square kilometers of Brazilian rainforest were destroyed in just one year.

Slashing and burning rainforests releases massive amounts of carbon dioxide into the atmosphere. This deforestation represents up to 75 percent of Brazil's total greenhouse gas emissions; Brazil is the fourth largest emitter of greenhouse gases, largely because of deforestation. Continued expansion of soybean farming will only lead to further destruction of the rainforest and more global warming. A recent report predicts that with a 1.7° Celsius increase in temperature, up to 45 percent of the plants in Brazil's Cerrado (central savannas) could become extinct by 2050. Unfortunately, it is projected that a 3.3° Celsius rise in temperature will occur within this century.

Some of the soybean plantations produce biofuel, and it is true that the development of the biofuel industry has opened up job possibilities for Brazilians who currently lack them. But one concern is that this type of industrial farming, or "monofarming," tends to push small-scale farmers off their land. Brazilian farmers who once farmed for food are now farming for fuel. A further economic concern is the financing behind other soybean plantations, which comes largely from outside of Brazil. Agribusiness corporations like Cargill are responsible for 60 percent of the financial investments in soybean production in Brazil. According to critics, these corporations are driving much of the deforestation of the Amazon as they finance the soy fed to chickens that are sold in supermarkets and fast-food restaurants across Europe.

B. DISCUSSION QUESTIONS

Work in groups. Discuss your answers to the questions.

1. Do you believe that a sustainable energy future is possible? Why or why not?

2. What are the political-economic relationships among land, people, resources, and food that Holt-Giménez refers to in discussing biofuels? Give examples.

A. GRAMMAR: Implied Conditions

Notice Read the following paragraphs from Eric Holt-Giménez's editorial. Focus on the boldfaced verb forms in the second paragraph. Is Holt-Giménez discussing real or unreal conditions here? What is the implied "*if* clause" in these statements?

> *Industrialized countries started the biofuels boom by demanding ambitious renewable-fuel targets. These fuels are to provide 10 percent of Europe's transport power by 2020. The United States wants 35 billion gallons a year.*
>
> *These targets far exceed the agricultural capacities of the industrial North. Europe* **would need to plant** *70 percent of its farmland with fuel crops. The entire corn and soy harvest of the United States* **would need to be processed** *as ethanol and biodiesel. Converting most arable land to fuel crops* **would destroy** *the food systems of the North, so the Organization of Economic Cooperation and Development countries are looking to the South to meet demand.*

Explanation Conditional sentences do not always state the condition. The subordinate clause ("*if* clause") is not always included when it is implied from the context. In the above example, Holt-Giménez is using the present unreal conditional. He is imagining what would happen if the goals of industrialized countries were realized. The implied "*if* clause" in his second paragraph is "If biofuel targets reached their goals . . ."

Exercise 1

Fill in the blanks with the correct form of the verbs in parentheses. Both active and passive verb forms are used.

1. The use of biofuels such as ethanol could begin to address the issue of global

   warming and climate change. Imagine what it _____ like now
                         (be)

   if most vehicles _____ on corn, soybeans, or palm oil instead
              (run)

   of fossil fuels? More crops _____, which _____
              (plant)   **(absorb)**

   more carbon dioxide from the atmosphere. Photosynthesis

   _____ more oxygen. The planet _____ greener.
     (produce)   **(be)**

2. Imagine that carbon dioxide_____ by burning fossil fuels.
              (not produce)

   The earth's atmosphere _____ cleaner today. We
              (be)

   _____ to grow plants for fuel. All of our crops
     (not need)

_____ for food rather than fuel. Biodiversity
(plant)

_____ rather than replacing small farms with single-crop
(maintain)

farming.

3. So far, a hydrogen economy has not been established. But suppose we

_____ in a world in which hydrogen can _____
(live)   (can / produce)

cheaply. Our energy sources _____. We _____ a
(never/run out)   (use)

sustainable energy to fuel our cars. The only byproduct of hydrogen

_____ water rather than carbon dioxide. We
(be)

_____ worry about geopolitical tensions in the Persian Gulf
(not need to)

or decreasing oil supplies.

Exercise 2

Write a paragraph similar to the ones in Exercise 1 in which you imagine what it would be like to live in a world without pollution and global warming.

B. WRITING STYLE: Refutation in Argumentative Writing

Notice   Notice the way Holt-Giménez develops his argument against the development of biofuels. How does he organize his different arguments?

Explanation   Holt-Giménez organizes his ideas according to the arguments that have been presented by the opposition, those who favor the development of biofuels. He then refutes the arguments of the opposition (which he calls "myths") by offering evidence to show that they are wrong.

Exercise 1

For each of the "myths" or arguments Holt-Giménez discusses, paraphrase his refutation in one sentence. Be sure to use your own words. The first one has been done for you.

Arguments Favoring Biofuels	Holt-Giménez's Refutation
1. Biofuels are clean and green.	*There are more emissions produced from biofuels than fossil fuels when we consider land preparation for growing them.*

Arguments Favoring Biofuels	Holt-Giménez's Refutation
2. Biofuels will not result in deforestation.	_____
	_____
3. Biofuels will bring rural development.	_____
	_____
4. Biofuels will not cause hunger.	_____
	_____

Exercise 2

In his commentary, Jeremy Rifkin makes several arguments in favor of a hydrogen-based economy. Read the following arguments. Imagine possible refutations that could be made by his opponents. Consider points made in the Background Reading as well as your own ideas. Write a statement that directly refutes each of his ideas.

Arguments Made by Rifkin in Favor of Hydrogen	Possible Refutation by His Opponents
1. Its [hydrogen's] impact will be as profound as the harnessing of coal and steam power in the nineteenth century and the oil-powered internal combustion engine in the twentieth century.	_____ _____ _____ _____
2. The space program was a collaborative effort, and it worked. Now we should set an equally ambitious goal of creating a fully integrated hydrogen economy by 2030.	_____ _____ _____ _____
3. What's required is a massive research and development commitment at the federal level, in the order of billions of dollars spread out over the next few decades.	_____ _____ _____

Arguments Made by Rifkin in Favor of Hydrogen	Possible Refutation by His Opponents
4. We should enlist the nation's federal laboratories and universities in every aspect of the effort, along with industry and civil institutions.	_____ _____ _____ _____
5. We should enact legislation at both the federal and state levels to provide special tax credits and other incentives to encourage start-up companies to stay in the field and established companies to enter the field.	_____ _____ _____ _____ _____ _____

C. ESSAY QUESTIONS

Write an essay on one of the numbered topics. Use ideas, vocabulary, and writing techniques from this unit. Try to incorporate the following:

- an introductory paragraph that presents both sides of the argument and clearly states your thesis
- paragraphs (at least three) that develop your argument with supportive evidence
- a conclusion that reinforces the position you have taken and ends with a new idea (a warning, prediction, value judgment) that has not been mentioned before

1. In his commentary on a hydrogen-based economy, Rifkin states: "For those who question whether we can afford all this, perhaps we should turn the question around and ask: How do we even begin to calculate the lost opportunity if we say no to a sustainable energy future and a third industrial revolution?"

   In contrast, Holt-Giménez, in the conclusion to his editorial, says: "A global moratorium on the expansion of biofuels is needed to develop regulatory structures and foster conservation and development alternatives to the transition. We need the time to make a better transition to food and fuel sovereignty."

Although Rifkin and Holt-Giménez are talking about different sources of alternative energy, they both refer to the government's role in moving forward. To what extent should governments control the future development of sustainable energy, in your opinion? Should more subsidies be given for a more rapid transition to alternative energy? Or should governments impose moratoriums in order to spend more time understanding the pros and cons of this transition? Write an essay in which you express your opinion.

2. Rifkin wants the United States to develop a crash program to achieve a hydrogen economy, but he says nothing about the impact on less-developed nations. Holt-Giménez makes clear the harmful effects of some American biofuel decisions on Brazil. What role should considerations of North-South problems have in deciding alternative energy choices?

NOTES

NOTES

NOTES